Pashto Grammar

Noor Ullah

authorHOUSE®

AuthorHouse™ UK Ltd.
500 Avebury Boulevard
Central Milton Keynes, MK9 2BE
www.authorhouse.co.uk
Phone: 08001974150

First published by AuthorHouse 5/16/2011

ISBN: 978-1-4567-8007-4 (sc)

Introductory Note:

"Some have described Afghanistan as a land in shadow. The same could be said for one of the country's official languages, Pashto. Many of the books written about this beautiful and yet elusive language are useful, but not practical; interesting, but not thorough; or unique to their time, but no longer current.

Noor Ullah's work serves to fill the gaps left by other attempts to clarify the grammar of the Pashto language. It provides a detailed overview of the main grammar points, uses current vocabulary and from the outset frames the language in principles essential to gaining a deep understanding of Pashto tense: aspect, stress, infection etc.

Whatever his or her aim, the learner will be well served by this much-needed guide to a language gradually stepping out from the shadows. "

Stuart,

05/10/2010, England

TABLE OF CONTENTS

The Pashto Alphabet
a) *Original Pashto Sounds*

Letter	Name	English Equivalent	Phonetic Symbol	Examples of Form		
				Initial	Medial	Final
ا	Alap	a/ aa	ă, a	ا اَتَل	ـا کار	ـا ستا
ب	Bé	B	b	بـ بل	ـبـ تمبل	ـب کب
پ	Pé	P	p	پـ پښتو	ـپـ ثپه	ـپ چپ
ت	Té	t, soft	t	تـ تؤر	ـتـ چتر	ـت اوچت
ټ	Tté	t, hard	ṭ	ټـ ټال	ـټـ خټه	ـټ کټ
ج	Jim	J	j	جـ جؤړ	ـجـ کجاوه	ـج کنج
ځ	Dzé	nearly dz	J	ځـ ځوان	ـځـ ښبځه	ـځ لمونځ
چ	Ché	Ch	Č	چـ چتر	ـچـ کچه	ـچ مچ
څ	Tsé	Nearly ts	C	څـ څلؤر	ـڅـ کڅؤړه	ـڅ کڅ
خ	Khé	Kh	X	خـ خپته	ـخـ مخه	ـخ مخ
د	Daal	d, soft	d	د دلته	ـد شیدي	ـد سد
ډ	Ddaal	d, hard	ḏ	ډ ډنګر	ـډ بډه	ـډ خنډ
ر	Ré	r, like in Spanish	r	ر رنګ	ـر ګرم	ـر مشر
ړ	Rré	rr, hard	ṛ	ړ ړنګ	ـړ ګړنګ	ـړ ربړ
ز	Zé	Z	z	ز زنګ	ـز مزی	ـز ربېز
ژ	Jé	as French jé	3	ژـ ژبه	ـژـ نیژدي	

ځ	Jjé	Je in western and gay in eastern dialect	Ź/ ğ	ځ ځيره	ـځ كـځـه	ـځ سپيځ
س	Sin	S	s	سـ سر	ـسـ خسر	ـس خس
ش	Shin	Sh	ʃ	شـ شل	ـشـ كشر	ـش تش
ښ	Sshin	sh in western and kh in western dialect	ş	ښـ ښار	ـښـ پښه	ـښ وينښ
غ	Ghain	Gh	γ	غـ غل	ـغـ پېغله	ـغ كتغ
ک	Kaap	K	k	کـ كور	ـکـ ليكه	ـیک ليک
ګ	Gaap	G	g	ګـ ګؤر	ـګـ مګر	ـګ تګ
ل	Laam	L	l	لـ لور	ـلـ پلؤر	ـل ختل
م	Mim	M	m	مـ مؤر	ـمـ كمر	ـم غنم
ن	Nun	N	n	نـ نرى	ـنـ پنر	ـن ستن
ڼ	Nunr	nr, hard	ŋ	-	ـڼـ گڼه	ـڼ گڼ
و	Waw	w, short	w, u	و ور	ـو سور	ـو ثو
ؤ	Wo	w, long	O	ؤ ؤر	ـؤ كؤر	ـؤ څلؤر
ه	Hé	H	h	هـ هلك	ـهـ بهر	
ه	Hé	A	a	-	-	ه/ـه سره/ښځه
ة	é	a	a	-	-	ة/ـة واده/ نيكة
ى	Yé	Ay	æ	-	-	سرى
ي	Yé	I	i	يـ يو	ـيـ سيند	ـي اولسي

Form	Name	English Equivalent	Phonetic Symbol	Initial	Medial	Final
ى	Yé	Ai	əy	–	–	ى اينجلى
ي	Yé	Ey	e	–	چـ مبله	ي بنځي
ئ	Yé	Ei	əy	–	–	ـئ راشئ
◌َ	Zwar	E	a	◌َ	◌َ	◌َ
ۀ/ـۀ	Zwarkai	a	ə			ۀ/ـۀ

b)   *Arabic sounds used in Pashto*

Form	Name	English Equivalent	Phonetic Symbol	Examples of Form		
				Initial	Medial	Final
ث		S	θ	ثـ ثواب	ـثـ اكثر	ـث بحث
ح		H	h	حـ حد	ـحـ بحر	ـح فتح
ذ		Z	δ	ذ ذكر	ـذ عذر	ـذ كاغذ
ص		S	S	صـ صمد	ـصـ مصر	ـص تخلص
ض		Z	z	ضـ ضد	ـضـ تضاد	ـض مرض
ط		T	t	ط طرف	ـطـ خطر	ـط خط
ظ		Z	z	ظ ظرف	ـظـ حفظان	ـظ حظ
ع		A	Σ	عـ عجب	ـعـ تعجب	ـع شمع
ف		F	f	فـ فرق	ـفـ تفرق	ـف نصف
ق		Q	q	قـ قدر	ـقـ تقدير	ـق شق

The Structure

Sentence Construction

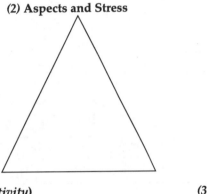

(2) Aspects and Stress

(1) **Inflection (*Ergativity*)**
  (Pronoun +Verb+ to be)

(3) Cases

Summary:

(1) Inflection:

In Pashto sentences, *to be* merges with the verb and inflects subject or object pronouns depending on the nature of the verb and tense. There are **four** main categories of verbs.

Pashto has an **Ergative** construction which is used with **transitive** verbs; that is the predicate fully or partly agrees with the object of the action which is put in the absolute case, whereas the subject/actor is in the oblique case.

(2) Aspect and Stress:

Every tense has two aspects, **perfective** and **imperfective**. Both affect the four main categories of the verb. In the former, the stress is applied on the **initial** part of verbs and in the latter the stress is applied on the **final** part of verbs.

(3) Cases:

There are <u>ten</u> cases in Pashto. Except a few, most of them are pre-postpositional in construction.

1. **Inflection** (the relationship among *Pronoun, Verb and to be*)

(I)   Pronouns

a)   See the following table:

Table 1

Pronouns				Person
Plural		Singular		
We	موږ	I	زه	1
You	تاسي	You	ته	2
They	دوی/هغوی	He	دی/هغۀ	3m
		She	دا/هغه	3f

b)   Pronouns and to *be* in Present and Past tense:
See the following table and compare it with table number 1:

Table: 2   Pronoun and to be

To be				Pronoun	Person
Past		Present			
I was	وم	I am	یم	زه	
We were	وو	We are	یو	موږ	1
You were	وي	You are	یي	ته	
You were	وئ	You are	یئ	تاسي	2
He was	وؤ	He is	وي(دی)	دی/هغۀ	
She was	وه	She is	وي(ده)	دا/هغه	3
They were (*pm*)	ول	They are	وي(دي)	دوی/هغوی	
They were (*pf*)	وې				

Note: All *to be* verbs have just **two** letters.

(II)   **Verb**

- All Pashto infinitives end in the letter of *L /ل/*.
- Pashto verbs fall into **two** main categories: (1) **Primitive** verbs and (2) **Derivative** verbs.

1) **Primitive Verbs:** These are the simple or original verbs ending **just** in /ل/ (L), such as چینبل، وتل، وهل، کول، کېدل. Thes verbs are limited in number.

2) **Derivative Verbs:** These are the compound verbs which have two segments, a noun/adjective and an auxiliary of a Primitive verb. Such as جلا، پوری added by کول، وتل: *جلاکول، پوری وتل*

   Derivative verbs are further divided into the following two different groups of compound verbs:

       (i)   **Compound** verbs of a noun/adjectives added **only** by Primitive verbs /کول-ول/ and /کېدل-بدل/ in *جلاکول and ویربدل*

       On the basis of **perfective** and **imperfective** aspects, these compound verbs are further divided into two sub groups:

       (a) Long compound verbs like, جلا کېدل، جلا کول/جوړول، جوړبدل

       (b) Short compound verbs: وېربدل، وېرول.

       (ii)   **Compound** verbs added by Primitive verbs **other** than /کېدل-بدل/ such as *پوری وهل، پوری وتل، کېنی ناستل* in وهل، وتل، ناستل These compound verbs are in limited number. Their form does not change in perfective and imperfective aspect. However, only the location of stress shifts from the adjectival part to the verbal part.

9

Sentence: The merger of (a) *to be* and (b) a verb

(a) *to be*

- Pashto sentences are formed by merging a verb with a conjubated form of *"to be"*
- During the merger the **first** of the two letters of a *to be* is dropped
- After the drop the *first* and *second* persons become similar in both present and past tenses while the *third* person remains different

See the following table and compare it with table number 2:

Table 3

To be (*Verbal Suffixes*)			Pronoun	Person
Past		**Present**		
	م	م	زه	
	و	و	موږ	1
	ې	ې	ته	
	ئ	ئ	تاسې	2
(MS) ؤ			ي	دی/هغۀ	
(FS) ه			ي	دا/هغه	3
(MP) ل			ي	دوی/هغوی	
(FP) ې					

(b) *Verb*

- During the merger the **final** /ل/ of the verb drops in the Present tense. It is optional but preferred in the Past tense

In the following table, see merger of the verbs چينبل and ختل in Present and Past tense respectively and compare it with table number 3:

10

Table 4

Merger of verb and to be		Pronoun	Person
Past ختل	**Present** چینبل		
I was climbing ختلــم	I am drinking چینبــم	زه	1
We were climbing ختلــو	We are drinking چینبــو	موږ	
You were climbing ختلــې	You are drinking چینبــې	ته	2
You were climbing ختلــئ	You are drinking چینبــئ	تاسې	
He was climbing ختلــؤ	He is drinking چینبــي	دی/هغۀ	3
She was climbing ختلــه	She is drinking چینبــي	دا/هغه	
They were climbing ختلــل	They are drinking چینبــي	دوی/هغوی	
They were climbing ختلــﺑ			

2. Aspect and Stress

In Pashto, every tense has *perfective* and *imperfective* aspects indicating the termination and continuity of an action respectively.

In both aspects the **stress** is applied to the verb. In the perfective, the stress is applied to the **initial** part of verbs, while in the imperfective it is applied to the **final** part of verbs

For details see in the following table the relationship between **aspects** and four main categories of **verb** in the present and past tense:

Table 5

Past		Present		Verb Category	No.
Imperfective (Final Stress)	**Perfective** (Initial Stress)	**Imperfective** (Final Stress)	**Perfective** (*Aorist*) (Initial Stress)		
No change	/و/ is prefixed	/ل/ is dropped	/و/ is prefixed /ل/ is dropped	**Primitive** Verb وهل	1
No change	/اکړل/ ➔ /اکول-ول/ /شول/ ➔ /اکبدل-بدل/	/ل/ is dropped, /اکېږ-ېږ/ ➔/اکبد -ېد /	/(کﭘ)کــ/ ➔ /اکول-ول/ /شــ/ ➔ /اکبدل-بدل/	**Long** Compound Verb خالي کول/جوړول خالي کېدل/جوړېدل	2
No change	/و/ is prefixed	/ل/ is dropped, /اﭘﮊ/ ➔ /اﭘﺪ /	/ل/ is dropped, /و/ is prefixed /اﭘﮊ/ ➔ /اﭘﺪ /	**Short** Compound Verbs وﭘﺮول/وﭘﺮېدل	3
The stress falls on the **latter** part of the verb	The stress falls on the **initial** part of the verb	/ل/ is dropped, The stress falls on the **latter** part of the verb.	/ل/ is dropped, The stress falls on the **initial** part of the verb.	**Shifting** Stress پوریﻰوهل	4

For further detail see the following table and compare it with table 5:

Table 6

Past		Present		Verb Category	No
Imperfective (Final Stress)	**Perfective** (Initial Stress)	**Imperfective** (Final Stress)	**Perfective** *(Aorist)** (Initial Stress)		
ما باجه وهله	ما باجه ووهله	زه باجه وهم	زه باجه و وهم	**Simple** وهل	1
ما کوټه خالي کوله زه خالي کېدلم ما کوټه جوړوله زه جوړېدلم	ما کوټه خالي کړله زه خالي شولم ما کوټه جوړه کړله زه جوړه شولم	زه خالي کوم زه خالي کېږم زه جوړوم زه جوړېږم	زه خالي کـم زه خالي شـم زه جوړ کـم زه جوړ شـم	**Long** Compound خالي کول/جوړول خالي کېدل/جوړېدل	2
ما پیشو وهروله زه وهرېدلم	ما پیشو ووهروله زه وهرېدلم	زه وهروم زه وهرېږم	زه و وهروم زه و وهرېږم	**Short** Compound وهرول/وهرېدل	3
ما دروازه پوري وهله	ما دروازه پوري وهله	زه پوري وهم	زه پوري وهم	**Shifting Stress** پوري وهل	4

3. Cases

For a detailed explanation of *Cases,* see page number 62

Pronouns

Pronouns can be classified as:

1. Personal
2. Oblique
3. Possessive
4. Weak
5. Demonstrative
6. Interrogative
7. Directive
8. Relative
9. Correlative
10. Indefinite
11. Negative
12. Reflexive

1. Personal Pronouns

Personal pronouns in Pashto can be divided three groups. Only the third person singular has masculine and feminine forms

Plural		Singular		Person
we	موږ	I	زه	1
you	تاسي	you	ته	2
they	دوی (هغوی)	he	دی(هغۀ)	3
		she	دا (هغه)	

The third person دی/دا/دوی refers to proximate positions and هغۀ/هغه/هغوی to remote ones

2. Oblique Pronouns

All direct singular personal pronouns in oblique cases change into the following forms:

Oblique	Direct
ما	زه
تا	ته
دۀ	دی
دې	دا
هغې	هغه
چا	څوک
کومي	کومه
څومي	څومه

13

3. Possessive Pronouns

In Pashto possessive pronouns are formed by adding the preposition / دَ / to independent personal pronouns in *oblique* case. In the first person this changes into /ز/; and in the second person it changes into /ـس/.

Plural		Singular		Person
our	زموږ (د موږ)	my	زما (دما)	1
your	ستاسي (د تاسي)	your	ستا (دتا)	2
their	دَ دوی / دَ هغوی	his	دَ دۀ / دَهغۀ	3
		her	دَ دي/ دَ هغي	

4. Weak Pronouns

The use of weak pronoun is more common in Pashto language. With transitive verbs, they can function as subject in the past tense, as object in the present and future tenses, and possessive pronouns in any tense and with form of verb. Weak pronouns never begin a sentence.

Possessive	Present (as *object*)	Past (as *subject*)	Weak Pronoun Plural	Weak Pronoun Singular	Person
our/ my	us / me	we / I	مو	مي	1
Your	You	You	مو	دي	2
his/her/its/their	him/her/it/them	he/she/it/they	يي	يي	3

5. Demonstrative Pronouns

Demonstrative pronouns are divided into four categories on the basis of the degree of the distance and remoteness, however, the forth degree is rarely used.

Degree of distance	Female	Male
1 Proximate (this)	دغه (هی/هیه)	دغۀ (دا) (هی)(هیه)
2 Remote (that)	هغه	هغۀ
3 Remoter (that)	هاغه(ها)	هاغۀ (ها)
4 Remotest (that)	هوغه	هوغۀ

6. Interrogative Pronouns

Meaning	Feminine	Masculine
Who	څوک	څوک
Which	کومه	کوم
which (for ordinal number)	څؤومه	څؤوم
What	څۀ	څۀ
How many	څو	څو
How much	څومرۀ	څومرۀ
How much	څونۀ	څونۀ
How	څرنگه/څرنگي	څرنگه

7. Directive Pronouns

The directive pronouns inflect only for person irrespective of their number and gender:

Directive Pronoun	Person
را	1
در	2
ور	3

They are combined with preposition and adverbs, e.g.:

ور	در	را	Preposition/ Verbs
with him/her/it/them ورسره	with you درسره	with me/us راسره	with سره
to him/her/it/them ورته	to you درته	to me/us راته	to ته
on him/her/it/them ورباندي	on you درباندي	on me/us راباندي	on باندي
to give him/her/it/them ورکول	to give you درکول	to give me/us راکول	کول

In addition to this, the use of ترې/ځيني: (from him/her/it/them) and پرې: (on him/her/it/them) is also very common. But they are used to refer to third person as **indirect object** only. e.g.:

I demand money from my father زه له پلار څخه پیسي غواړم

(زه پیسې ځيني/ترې غواړم)

I keep books on the table زه په مېز باندي کتابونه ږدم

زه کتابونه پرې ږدم

15

8. Relative Pronouns

In Pashto, the conjunction /چي/is functions as a relative pronoun which joins two finite sentences. It can be for "that", "when", "because", "as", "if", "whether", "while", and "lest" etc.

I want to sleep	زه غواړم چي ويده شم
Take some medicine, if you are sick.	ته دومل وَخوره چي رنځوريې
Atal is the man who is a Doctor in the village	اتل هغه سړی دی چي په کلي کښي ډاکتر دی
This is the man whose name is *Atal*	دغه هغه سړی دی چي نوم يې اتل دی
This is the book for which I am searching.	دغه هغه کتاب دی چي زه يې لټوم

9. Correlative Pronouns

In Pashto /که/ (if) and /چي/ (that), and interrogative pronouns combined with /چي/ and afterwards added by /نو/, /خو/, /دومره/, /هغسي/ etc. are used as correlative pronouns.

If you are hungry, (so) eat the food.	که ته وږي يې نو ډوډۍ وَخوره.
(If) you are hungry you (should) eat the food.	چي وږی يې خو ډوډۍ وَخوره.
When I became hungry, (then) I ate the food.	کله چي زه وږی شوم نو ما ډوډۍ وَخوړله
Eat as much as you like.	څومره چي ته غواړي هغومره ډوډۍ وَخوره
Do as you wish.	څنګه چي ستا خوښه وي هغسي کار کوه
Whoever you like, invite him/her/them.	څوک چي ستا خوښ وي هغه راوَبوله

10. Indefinite Pronouns

one/ any one	يو
another	بل
another one	بل يو
every one	هر يو
others	نور
all	ټول
all	واړه
some	څه /يوڅه
some	څينۀ/څيني
some one	څوک /يوڅوک
some	څو /يوڅو
any	کوم/کوم يو؟کوم څوک

16

11. Negative Pronouns

nothing	هیڅ:
nothing	هیڅ شی:
no one	هیڅ څوک :

12. Reflexive Pronouns

one's (self/selves)	پخپله:
self	ځان:
one's self	دَ خپل ځان لپاره:

Nouns

1 Important forms of Noun

In Pashto, the following five forms of Nouns are very important because of their peculiar structure:

1) Verbal Noun (Gerund), 2) Abstract Noun, 3) Mass Noun, 4) Diminutive Nouns

1) Verbal Nouns:

- All infinitives can be used as masculine plural nouns (Gerunds). e.g. hitting, making, scaring, sitting etc, وهل، جوړول، وبرول، کښېناستل

- Gerunds can be made by replacing the final /ل/ of any infinitive by /نگ/. These nouns are masculine singular.
  Examples: وهنگ، جوړونگ، وبربدنگ، کښېناستنگ

- Masculine plural nouns can be formed from intransitive verbs by replacing the final /ل/ with /ۀ/ and Feminine singular by replacing the final /ل/ by /ا/
  Examples: جوړېدۀ، وبربدۀ، کښېناستۀ
  جوړېدا، وبربدا، کښېنستا

2) Abstract Nouns
Generally formed by adding ون، گلوي، ي، توب، تیا، والي، ينت to nouns and adjectives:
Examples: لوی=لوینت، لوی والی، هوښیار=هوښیارتیا، هوښیارتوب، هوښیاري، ورورگلوي، ژوندون
life, brotherhood, clerveness, greatness

17

3) **Mass Nouns**

Those nouns which are only used as plural, as:

اوبه، غوړي، تبل، شيدې، مستې، کوچ،شراب، چرس، کوکنار، ډيزل، پيټرول، ګريس، (او نور)

4) **Diminutive Nouns**

These nouns are formed by adding ګی/اګی، ګوتی/اګوتې،ی/ئ، تی/اتی، کی/اکی/اکې

Examples:

ټنارګی/بسوګی، ، ټنارګوتی/ ، اناری/کشمالی، زلموتی/ پيغلوتې، ځوانکی/ ځوانکی/ اورکی

In Pashto Nouns, the following three features are very important:

1. **Gender**: (a) Feminine (b) Masculine
2. **Numbers**: (a) Singular (b) Plurals
3. **Cases**: Nominative, Accusative, Vocative, Genitive, Dative, Ablative, Locative, Instrumental

1. *Gender*

(a) Endings of Feminine Nouns

Nouns ending in ۍ، ي، ی، ه، ا are feminine; however, there are a few exceptions. See the following table:

Exceptions	Example	Ending Sound
	نجلۍ، رسۍ، ډوډۍ، شپېلۍ، هوسۍ، ښپلۍ،چوکۍ...	ۍ
	ادي، اغلي، خواښي،ناوي، ملګري، روي، سَندرغاړي، سترګي...	ي
Nouns of *profession:* موچي،نايي، ،سخي..	دوښمني ، دوستي، خوشحالي، خپَلوي، آزادي...	ي in Abstract Nouns
بابا، ماما، لالا، کاکا، مَلا، سندرا	امريکا، کاناډا، اسيا، نخا، بلا، ملا، ليلا...	ا
	ښځه، پانه، غرمه، منه، سترګه، پنبه، ونه، توره...	ه
Some diminutives: سدؤ، کاکو، جمالؤ، لالؤ... *All oblique plurals:* (دَ) پنبتنؤ، سرؤ، ښځؤ...	پَنبتؤ، وَرشؤ، بيزؤ، لامبؤ، راډيؤ، زانګؤ...	ؤ in direct singular nouns
	مؤر، خؤر، ترؤر، لور، يور، نبؤر،ندرؤر،	Kinship nouns ending in consonants

18

(b) Endings of Masculine Nouns

Nouns ending in <u>consonants</u> and <u>vowels</u>, و، ة and diphthong ی are Masculine, though there a few exceptions. See the following table:

Exceptions	Example	Ending Sound
The colloquial* لار، ورځ، مياشت، خُرمن، ځنلگل،لوبښت،مت،وريځ، برستن، ږمنځ، لمن،ستن، کتو ،مبڅن،ترښ، غبر، منگول، خپر، مهرمن، بن، تپندار، مبر	کتاب، مېز، دېوال، لاس،غوږ...	*All Consonants*
	سری، زمری، پسرلی، دوبی، لرگی، لیونی...	*Diphthong* ی
Abstract Nouns: دوستي، خوشحالي، دوښمني	قاضي، موچي،سخي،نايي،مرکچي،لندارچي، تازي، ښاري ...	*ي in nouns of profession*
	چاکو، پتو، زردالو، شَفتالو،سالو...	*Short* و
	لو، پلو، کندَو، سيلاو، پراو، کراو، ...	*Diphthong* و
	زړۀ، ترۀ،ورارۀ،نيکۀ، پسۀ،لېوۀ،مرغۀ،کارغۀ	ۀ

* In standard form all these nouns end in /ه/:

لاره، ورڅه، مياشته، خُرمنه، ځنگله،لوبښته، مته، برستنه،ږمنځه، لمنه،ستنه، کتوه ، مبڅنه، ترښبه، غبر،منکوله، خپره، مهرمنه،بنه، تپندراه، مبره

2. Number

The formation of Plural Nouns

(a)   Plurality of *Feminine* Nouns:

Examples	Changes in Plurality	Ending Sound in Singular
خندا= خنداگانې/خنداوې، ژرا= ژراگانې/ژراوې، غوا= غواگانې/غواوې...	Add /گانې/ or /وې/	ا
ښځه= ښځې، ونه= ونې، سترگه= سترگې، تخته= تختې، رمه= رمې...	/ه/ is replaced by /ې/	ه
کړکۍ=کړکۍ/کړکیانې، خولۍ=خولۍ/خولیانې، څپلۍ= څپلۍ /څپلیانې، دوډۍ= دوډۍ/دوډیانې...	Remains unaltered or /انې/ is added.	ۍ
دوستي=دوستۍ/دوستیانې، خوشحالي=خوشحالۍ/خوشحالیانې، خواري= خوارۍ/ خواریانې، څپلوي= څپلوۍ/څپلویانې، ناروغي=ناروغۍ/ناروغیانې...	/ۍ/ is replaced by /انې/ or /ۍ/ is added	ي in Abstract nouns
اغلې= اغلې، ملگرې= ملگرې، روپ= ملگرې، سّندرغارې = سندرغارې...	No alteration, except /ادې/ادې/ گانې، خواښې=خواښیانې، ناوې=ناویانې	ې
بیزو=بیزوگانې، ورشو=ورشوگانې، راډیو=راډیوگانې، زانگو=زانگوگانې	/گانې/ is added	و

20

(b)   Plurality of *Masculine* Nouns

Examples	Changes for Plurality	Ending Sound
هلک=هلکان، پرانگ=پرانگان، اوبښ=اوبښان، اس=اسان (Animate) ------------------- مېز=مېزونه، کتاب=کتابونه، قلم=قلمونه، سیند=سیندونه (Inanimate)	*Animate* nouns are added by /ان/ while *inanimate* nouns by /ونه/	*All Consonants*
غل=غلۀ، مل=ملۀ، شین=شنۀ، سور=سرۀ، خر=خرۀ...	/ۀ/ is added	*Monosyllable*
1- پښتون=پښتانۀ، پوخ=پاخۀ، تؤد=تاودۀ، سؤر=سارۀ، زؤر=زارۀ... 2- لمونځ=لمنخونۀ، پتون=پتنونۀ، ورون=ورنونۀ، پتلون=پتلنونۀ، 3- تریو=تروۀ، تریخ=ترخۀ	1- /و/ is replace by /ا/ and /ۀ/ is added; 2- /و/ is dropped and /ونۀ/ is added; 3- /ی/ is dropped and /ۀ/ is added	*Ablaut*
ستوری=ستوري، غری=غرِي، لوبني=لوبنِي، ملگری=ملگرِي کابلی=کابلي/کابلیان، لمسی=لمسي/لمسیان، لپونی=لپونِي/لپونیان، زمری=زمري/زمریان...	Generally ی is replaced by ِي however some times /ان/ can be added	*Diphthong ی*
قاضي=قاضیان، موچي=موچیان، سخي=سخیان، نایي=نایان، مرکچي=مرکچیان، لندارچي=لندارچیان، تازي=تازیان، بناري=بناریان...	/ان/ is added	ي *in nouns of profession*
چاکو=چاکوگان/چاکوان، پَتو=پتوگان/پتوان، شفتالو=شفتالوگان/شفتالان...	گان is added	*Short و*
لو=لوونه، پَلو=پَلوونه، کنډو=کنډوونه، پَراو=پراوونه...	/ونه/ is added	*Diphthong و*
ترۀ=ترونه، ورارۀ=ورپرونه، پسۀ=پسونه، زړۀ=زړونه، ------------------- لپوۀ=لپوان، مرغۀ=مرغان، وبښتۀ=وبښتان	In some cases it is replaced by ونه while in others by ان	ۀ
نیکۀ=نیکگان/نیکونۀ، پلار=پلرونۀ/پلاران، مبرۀ=مبرونۀ، مور=مندې، خور=خوندي، نږوﺭ=نږندي، ندروﺭ=ندرندي، زوی=زامن، لور=لونې/لورگانې، وروﺭ=ورونۀ، ترۀ/ترونۀ، تروﺭ=ترندي، توربور=توربرونه/تربوران، ورارۀ=ورپرونۀ، لپور=لپورونۀ، یؤر=یونې، نجلی=نجونې/ جینی=جینکی	Mostly irregularly pluralized	*Consanguinity*
پینځۀ=ﺩالرۀ، اتۀ-پونډۀ، کالۀ، گزۀ، منۀ، سپرۀ، میلۀ، جریبۀ، اېکړۀ، ساعتۀ...	ۀ is added	*Number and measurement together*

Note: *In Pashto, mass nouns both as feminine and masculine are always plural:*
درمل، واکسین، ویتامین، اینتي بیوتیک، هیروین، چرس، بنگ، تمباکو، نسوار، غنم، جوار، زر، تپل، کوچ، غوړي، دیزل، پیټرول، اورۀ، اوبه، مستې، شپدي...

21

Ergative Construction

Ergative construction is used in the past tense of a transitive verb; the **predicate** agrees in person, number and gender with the **direct** (absolute) object, and subject changes into *oblique* case.

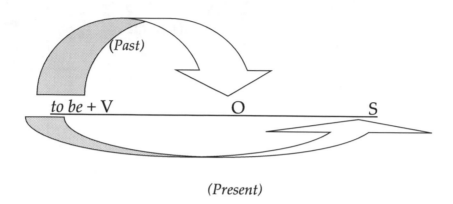

(Present)

Past										Present	
• to be agrees with object										to be	
• object *absolutive*										agreement	
• subject *oblique*										with subject	
دوی	دوی	دا	دی	تاسي	ته	موږ	زه				
وهلې	وهل	وهله	وهلؤ	وهلئ	وهلې	وهلو	وهلم	ما	هغه وهم	زه
								موږ	هغه وهو	موږ
								تا	هغه وهي	ته
								تاسي	هغه وهئ	تاسي
								دۀ	هغه وهي	دی
								دې	هغه وهي	دا
								دوی	هغه وهي	دوی

For furthe detail see the following talbe:

Past	Present
ما ډوډۍ وَخوړله	زه ډوډۍ وَخورم
ما ډوډۍ خوړله	زه ډوډۍ خورم
پلوشې سندرې وَ ويلې	پلوشه سندرې وَايي
سرې کتاب لوستلؤ	سرې کتاب لولي
پښتانۀ انگريزي زده کوله	پښتون انگريزي زده کوي
نبخې کور پاک کړؤ	نبخه کور پاکوي
هلک کوټه پاکه کړه	هلک کوټه پاکه* کي

22

*LCV and Present tense:

In **Present** tense, the adjectival/nominal component of a **transitive long compound verb** always agrees with the **object**. On the contrary, the auxiliaryy, /کول/, agrees with the **subject**

See the long verbs /ښکلی کول، تیارول، پاکول/ in the following table:

Past tense	Present tense

(_Integral_ agreement with the _object_)	_Split_ agreement of:
	  a) _Adjective – object_
	  b) _auxiliary – subject_

تا <u>کوټه پاکه کړه</u> سړي <u>دوډۍ تیاره کړه</u> ښځې <u>خوراک تیار کړؤ</u> تاسي <u>کور ښکلی کړؤ</u> اینجلئ <u>کورونه ښکلي کول</u> ما <u>کورونه ښکلي کول</u> موږ <u>کوټه ښکلي کوله</u>	ته <u>کوټه پاکه</u> کي سړی <u>دوډۍ تیاره</u> کي ښځه <u>خوراک تیار</u> کي تاسي <u>کور ښکلی</u> کئ اینجلۍ <u>کورونه ښکلي</u> کوي زه <u>کورونه ښکلي</u> کوم موږ <u>کوټه ښکلي</u> کوو

Weak Pronouns

Weak Pronouns		Person
Plural	Singular	
ا	مي	*1*
	دي	*2*
یــــــــي		*3*

1. Weak pronouns are used only with *transitive* verbs
2. Weak pronouns cannot begin a sentence
3. Weak pronouns are used as substitute of (i) *subject*, (ii) *object* and (iii) *possessive* pronouns;

(i) They are used as *subjects* in the Past tenses (agentive case), as in these tenses the personal endings already agree with the (*object*) of the sentence.

(ii) In the Present/Future, tense they are used as *objects* (accusative case) because the personal endings already agree with the (*subject*) of the sentence.

(iii) Weak pronouns as *Possessive* pronouns are used in all tenses and with all kinds of verbs.

For detail see the following tables:

Possessive	Past (as *Subject*)	Past (as *Object*)	Weak Pronouns		Person
			Plural	Singular	
our/ my	we / I	us/me	مـــو	مي	*1*
Your	You	You		دي	*2*
his/her/its/their	he/she/it/they	him/her/them	یــــي		*3*

Possessive		Past		Present		Person
Weak Pronoun	Strong Pronoun	Weak Pronoun	Strong Pronoun	Weak Pronoun	Strong Pronoun	
کورمي	زماکور	هغه مي وهله	ما هغه وهله	هغه مي وهي	هغه ما وهي	*1*
کور مو	زمورِ کور	هغه مو وهله	مورِ هغه وهله	هغه مو وهي	هغه مورِ وهي	
کور دي	ستاکور	هغه دي وهله	تا هغه وهله	هغه دي وهي	هغه تا وهي	*2*
کور مو	ستاسي کور	هغه مو وهله	تاسي هغه وهله	هغه مو وهي	هغه تاسي وهي	
کور یي	دَ دهٔ کور	هغه یي وهله	دهٔ هغه وهله	هغه دی وهي	هغه دی وهي	*3*
کور یي	دَ دي کور	هغه یي وهله	دي هغه وهله	هغه یي وهي	هغه دا وهي	
کور یي	دَ دوی کور	هغه یي وهله	دوی هغه وهله	هغه یي وهي	هغه دوی وهي	

24

Location of Weak Pronouns
As mentioned above, weak pronouns cannot begin a sentence, rather they need a host. The host they make from whatever other element appears initially to them in the sentence. In other words, weak pronouns always take the second position in the sentence.

(a)   Past Tense

<u>Strong Pronoun</u>

(Yesterday I did not eat the read.) ما پرون‌دودی، و نۀ خوړله

<u>Weak Pronoun</u>

پرون‌مي دودی، وَنۀ خوړله --------------

دودی مي وَنۀ خوړله --------------

وَمي نۀ خوړله --------------

وَمي خوړله --------

خوړله‌مي

(I was eating it)

(b)   Present Tense

<u>Strong</u>

<u>Pronoun</u>

(should) I not eat food today زه نن‌دودی، وَنۀ خورم

<u>Weak Pronoun</u>

زه یې نن وَنۀ خورم --------------

نن یې وَنۀ خورم --------------

وَیې نۀ خورم --------------

وَیې خورم --------

خورم یې

(I am eating it)

25

Weak Pronoun and the use of four main verbs:

(1)/وهل/ , (2)/جوړول/ , (3)/رنگول/ , (4)/کښېنول/

Past		Present	
Imperfective	Perfective	Imperfective	Perfective
سړي باجه نۀ وهله باجه يې نۀ وهله نۀ يې وهله وهله يې	سړي باجه وَ نۀ وهله باجه يې وَ نۀ وهله وَ يې نۀ وهله وَ يې وهله وهله يې	سړی باجه نۀ وهي سړی يې نۀ وهي نۀ يې وهي وهي يې	سړی باجه وَ نۀ وهي سړی يې وَ نۀ وهي وَ يې نۀ وهي وَ يې وهي وهي يې
ما کوټه نۀ جوړوله کوټه مي نۀ جوړوله نۀ مي جوړوله جوړوله مي	ما کوټه جوړه نۀ کړه کوټه مي جوړه نۀ کړه جوړه مي نۀ کړه جوړه مي کړه جوړوم يې	زۀ کوټه جوړه نۀ کوم زۀ يې نۀ جوړوم نۀ يې جوړوم جوړوم يې	زۀ کوټه جوړه نۀ کم زۀ يې جوړه نۀ کم چوړه يې نۀ کم جوړه يې کم جوړوم يې
ما کوټه نۀ رنگوله کوټه مي نۀ رنگوله نۀ مي رنگوله رنگوله مي	ما کوټه وَ نۀ رنگوله کوټه مي وَ نۀ رنگوله وَ مي نۀ رنگوله وَ مي رنگوله رنگوله مي	زۀ کوټه وَ نۀ رنگوم زۀ يې نۀ رنگوم نۀ يې رنگوم رنگوم يې	زۀ کوټه وَ نۀ رنگوم زۀ يې وَ نۀ رنگوم وَ يې نۀ رنگوم وَ يې رنگوم رنگوم يې
تاسي الوتکه نۀ کښېنوله الوتکه مو نۀ کښېنوله نۀ مو کښېنوله کښېنوله مو	تاسي الوتکه کښېنۀ نوله الوتکه مو کښېنۀ نوله کښېنۀ مو نوله کښېنۀ مو نوله کښېنوله مو	تاسي الوتکه نۀ کښېنوئ تاسي يې نۀ کښېنوئ تاسي يې کښېنوئ کښېنوئ يې	تاسي الوتکه کښېنۀ نوئ تاسي يې کښېنۀ نوئ کښېنۀ يې نۀ نوئ کښېنۀ يې نوئ کښېنوئ يې

26

Directive Pronouns

The directive pronouns /پري/،/تري/،/اور/، /ادر/، /ارا/ specify the course and direction of an action *towards, for, to, from and on* a particular person; the first three are used irrespective of gender and plurality

However, the latter two, /تري/ and /پري/, perform the combined function of preposition and direction and are used only for the 3rd person:

تري = from (him/her/them/it)

پري = on (him, her, them, it)

They are used in two slightly different forms:

a) As a preposition and suffixed by different postpositions, e.g. راته، درته، ورته. In this form the direction of a directive pronoun is dependent of the direction of the postpositions: for, to, from, on etc.

b) As a prefix and part of an infinitive. Mostly they are not part of the verbs, but in some instances, they are inseparable part of verbs, e.g. ورکول، درکول، راکول

For details see the following tables:

To (with infinitive)	On (with)	From	For (to)	Person
راکول to give me/us	on me/us راباندي	from me/us راخخه، رانه	for me/us(راله)(راته/رالره)	1
درکول to give you	on you درباندي	from you درخخه، درنه	(درته/درلره(درله) for you	2
ورکول to give to him/her/them/it	ورباندي on him/her/them/it	ورخخه، ورنه from him/her/them/it	ورته/ورلره(ورله) for him/her/them/it	3
	پري (بي)(پر) (به) on (by) him/her/them/it	تري (تربنه)(تي)/ څيني from him/her/them/it		

Complex structure:

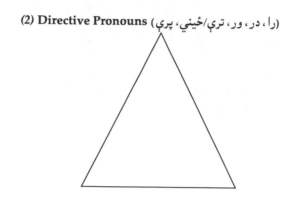

(2) Directive Pronouns (را، در، ور، تری/ځینې، پرې)

(1) Weak Pronoun
(می، دی، مو، یې)

(3) Action (Verb)

When weak pronouns together with Directive pronouns interact with verbs of different categories, the sentence morphs into short but difficult composition and becomes very difficult especially for the non-native speakers of Pashto.

Examples:

(1). ما له هغه څخه ستا لپاره په سايکل باندي ډوډۍ راوړه
(I brought the bread from him for you on the byke)

له هغه څخه مي ستا لپاره په سايکل باندي ډوډۍ راوړه.
له هغه څخه مي درته په سايکل باندي ډوډۍ راوړه.
له هغه څخه مي درته پرې ډوډۍ راوړه.
ډوډۍ مي ځينې پرې راوړه درته
ځينې را مي وړه پرې درته

(راله را يې وړه ترې!)

(2). زه له وني څخه دَ ځان لپاره په چاکو باندي منې راپرې کم؟
Shall I pluck apples with a knife for myself?

زه يې له وني څخه دَ ځان لپاره په چاکو باندي راپرې کم؟
له وني څخه يې دَ ځان لپاره په چاکو باندي را پرې کم؟
دَ ځان لپاره يې ترې په چاکو باندي راپرې کم؟
په چاکو باندي يې راپرې کم ترې؟
پرې راپرې يې کم ترې؟
(يې راپرې يې کم ځينې؟)

28

Verbs and Tenses

(1) Simple Verbs
(a) Intransitive and (b) Transitive

(a) Intransitive
- In Pashto, the number of intransitive simple verbs is the smallest
- All simple intransitive verbs except لیشل and درومل are irregular in Present tense
- Only را/ور/درتلل and تلل،کیدل are irregular in Past perfective

Formation of Tense:

Example: /وتل/

1. **Perfective:**

	be	+	verb	+	/و/	+	Subject
Present:	م ----------- وخــ				و		زه
Past:	م ----------- وتلــ				و		زه

2. **Imperfective:**

	be	+	verb	+	Subject
Present:	م ----------- وخــ				زه
Past:	م ----------- وتلــ				زه

Simple (*Intransitive*) Verbs

Be	Past		Present		Subject	Meaning	Verb
Past / Present	*Imperfective*	*Perfective*	*Imperfective*	*Perfective*			
(1st) S: م... P: و...	کېدل	شول	ـکېږ	شـ	زه مونږ ته تاسې دی دوی	to be/ become	کېدل
	تلل	ولاړ	ـځـ	ولاړش		to go	تلل
(2nd) S: ې... P: ئ...	را/اور/درغلـ	را/اور/در تلـ	را/اور/در ځـ	را/اور/در ش		to go to some one	را/اور/در تلل
	وتلـ	وتلـ	وځـ	وځـ		to exit	وتل
	ختلـ	ختلـ	ـخېژ	ـخېژ		to climb	ختل
(3rd) SM: ـي / ـؤ SF: ـي / ـه PM: ـي / ـل PF: ـي / ـې	پرتلـ	پرتلـ	پرځـ	پرځـ		To fall/tumble	پرتل
	الوتلـ	الوتلـ	الوځـ	الوځـ		to fly	الوتل
	اوښتلـ	اوښتلـ	اوړ	اوړ		to turn/ climb over	اوښتل
	نښتلـ	نښتلـ	نښلـ	نښلـ		to get stuck	نښتل
	رغبنتلـ	رغبنتلـ	رغړ	رغړ		to role over	رغبنتل
	رخبنتلـ	رخبنتلـ	رخړ	رخړ			رخبنتل
	وسَستلـ	وسَستلـ	وسلـ	وسلـ		to burst	وسَستل
	چولـ	چولـ	چو	چو		to burst	چول/چاودل
	لېنبلـ	لېنبلـ	لېنبـ	لېنبـ		to transfer	لېنبل
							لوشتل
			دروم	دروم		to go	درومل
	مړشولـ	مړکېدلـ	مر	مر		to die	مرل/مړکېدل

Note: The verbs تلل, مرل and را/در/ورتلل are used as compound verbs in present and past perfective that is why they don't take /و/.

(b) Transitive

- The number of simple transitive verbs is also limited
- Most of the transitive verbs are **regular** except a few
- The are nly irregular in Past perfective

Formation of Tense:

Example: /چينبل/

1. Perfective:

be + verb	+	/و/ +	Object	+	Subject

Present:	چينب‑‑‑‑‑‑م	و	اوبه	زه
Past:	چينب‑‑‑‑‑‑لې	و	اوبه	ما

2. Imperfective:

be	+	verb	+	Object	Subject

Present:	چينب‑‑‑‑‑‑م	شيدې	زه
Past:	چينب‑‑‑‑‑‑لې	شيدې	ما*

* In Past tense of a transitive verb all direct singular pronouns change into the *oblique* form:

زه = ما،   ته = تا،   دی = دۀ،   دا = دې

Simple (*Transitive*) Verbs

Be Past/Present	Past Imperfective	Past Perfective	Object	Subject	Present Imperfective	Present Perfective	Subject	Meanings	Verb
(1st) S: م P: و	کول	کول	(و) زه	ما	کو-	کو-	(و) زه	to do	کول
	کړل	کړل	موږ	موږ	کپ-	کپ-	موږ	to do	کړل
(2nd) S: ې P: ئ	خوړل	خوړل	ته	تا	خور-	خور-	ته	to eat	خوړل
	ژویل	ژویل	تاسې	تاسې	ژوپ	ژوپ	تاسې	to chew	ژوول
	چیچل	چیچل	دی	ده	چیچ	چیچ	دی	to bite	چیچل
	چینل	چینل	دوی	دوی	چینب	چینب	دوی	to drink	چینل
(3rd) SM: ؤ / ي SF: ه / ي PM: ل / ي PF: ې / ي	څکل	څکل	دا دوی	دې دوی	څک	څک	دا دوی	to taste	څکل
	وهل	وهل			وه-	وه-		to beat	وهل
	کوتل	کوتل			کوت-	کوت-		To crush	کوتل
	ترتل	ترتل			ترت-	ترت-		to scold	ترتل
	نتل	نتل			نت	نت		to drive away	نتل
	اسکړل	اسکړل			اسکړ-	اسکړ-		to scold	اسکړل
	کینل	کینل			کین-	کین-		to scold	کینل
	ښکنځل	ښکنځل			ښکنځ	ښکنځ		to swear at	ښکنځل
	تړل	تړل			تړ-	تړ-		to tie	تړل
	تپل	تپل			تپ-	تپ-		to impose	تپل
	کتل	کتل			گور-	گور-		to look	کتل
	لیدل	لیدل			وین-	وین-		to see	لیدل
	کسل	کسل			کس-	کس-		to look	کسل
	څارل	څارل			څار-	څار-		to observe	څارل
	کښل	کښل			کاږ-	کاږ-		to draw/ write	کښل
	لوستل/	لوستل/			لول-/لون-	لول/لون		to read/ to spread	لوستل
	گرځل	گرځل			گیرځ-	گیرځ-		to sreach	گیرځل
	ویل	ویل			وای-	وای-		to tell	ویل
	غوښتل	غوښتل			غواړ-	غواړ-		to demand/ want	غوښتل
	بلل	بلل			بول-	بول-		to call	بلل
	گڼل	گڼل			گڼ-	گڼ-		to count	گڼل
	شمېرل	شمېرل			شمېر-	شمېر-		to count	شمېرل
	پوښتل	پوښتل			پوښت-	پوښت-		to ask	پوښتل
	منل	منل			من-	من-		to accept	منل
	ایستل	ایستل			باس-	باس-		to expell	ایستل
	ساتل	ساتل			سات-	سات-		to keep	ساتل
	سپارل	سپارل			سپار-	سپار-		to give	سپارل
	وړل	وړل			یوس-	یوس-		to take/ carry	وړل

لېږل	to send	لېږ-	لېږ-			لېږل	لېږل
ښئیل	to show	ښیی-	ښیی-			ښیېل	ښیېل
ګنډل	to sew	ګنډ-	ګنډ-			ګنډل	ګنډل
نغښتل	to wrap	نغاړ-	نغاړ-			نغښتل	نغښتل
پېچل	to twist	پېچ-	پېچ-			پېچل	پېچل
پېژندل	to know	پېژن-	پېژن-			پېژند	پېژندل
پېيل	to thread	پېی-	پېی-			پېيل	پېيل
تومبل	to pin	تومب-	تومب-			تومبل	تومبل
اوبدل	to weave	اوب-	اوب-			اوبدل	اوبدل
سکڼتل	to design	سکڼ-	سکڼ-			سکڼتل	سکڼتل
کچل	to gauge	کچ-	کچ-			کچل	کچل
مېچل	to measrue	مېچ-	مېچ-			مېچل	مېچل
اوډل	to order	اوډ	اوډ			اوډل	اوډل
اوبدل	to weave	اوب-	اوب-			اوبدل	اوبدل
تلل	to waigh	تل	تل			تلل	تلل
داغل	to mark	داغ-	داغ-			داغل	داغل
مېنځل/وينځل	to wash	مينځ- وينځ-	مينځ- وينځ-			مېنځل/وينځل	مېنځل/وينځل
ولل	to wash	؟؟	؟؟			؟؟؟	؟؟؟
شاربل	to churn	شارب-	شارب-			شاربل	شاربل
خرېيل	to shave	خرېی-	خرېی-			خرېيل	خرېيل
تراشل	to trim	تراش-	تراش-			تراشل	تراشل
توړل	to erode	توړ-	توړ-			توړل	توړل
څوکرېيل	to cut	څوکرېی-	څوکرېی-			څوکرېيل	څوکرېيل
پرېړل	to cut	پرېړ-	پرېړ-			پرېړل	پرېړل
څېرل	to tear	څېر-	څېر-			څېرل	څېرل
لرل	to have	لر-	لر-			لرل	لرل
موښل/مږل	to rubb	موښ- مږ-	موښ- مږ-			موښل/مږل	موښل/مږل
اخنبل	to knead	اغب-	اغب-			اخنبل	اخنبل
کرل	to grow	کر-	کر-			کرل	کرل
ربېل	to reap	رب-	رب-			ربېل	ربېل
کپل	to count bad as a omen	کپ-	کپ-			کپل	کپل
وژل	to kill	وژن-	وژن-			وژل	وژل
وېشتل	to shoot	ول-	ول-			وېشتل	وېشتل
پانبل	to spread	پانب-	پانب-			پانبل	پانبل
موندل	to find	موند/موم-	موند/موم-			موندل	موندل
ګالل	to suffer	ګال-	ګال-			ګالل	ګالل

					Pashto	English	Pashto
زغمـ	زغمـ			زغمـ	زغمـ	to tolerate	زغمل
سهـ	سهـ			سهـ	سهـ	to absorb	سهل
وبشـ	وبشـ			وبش	وبش	to divide	وبشل
نیوـ	نیوـ			نیسـ	نیسـ	to hold	نیول
پوښـ	پوښـ			پوښـ	پوښـ	to cover	پوښل
اغوستـ	اغوستـ			اغوند	اغوند	to wear	اغوستل
کیندل/ کنستل/کنل	کیندل/ کنستل/کنل			کیند/کنـ	کیند/کنـ	to dig	کیندل/ کنستل/کنل
خرل	خرل			خرـ	خرـ	to dig	خرل
لمانځل	لمانځل			لمانځـ	لمانځـ	to celeberate	لمانځل
گومارل	گومارل			گومار	گومار	to appoint	گومارل
چنل	چنل			چنـ	چنـ	to filter	چنل
ټاکل	ټاکل			ټاک	ټاک	to select	ټاکل
پتپیل	پتپیل			پتپیـ	پتپیـ	to plan	پتپیل
						to coat	اخپل
						to feel nausce	اغپل

(2) Structure of Long-Compound Verb

- In Pashto long-compound verbs are the most common
- Long-compound verbs have two parts: *adjectival* (some times a noun) and auxiliary /کبدل/ or /کول/
- /کول/ makes transitive and/کبدل/ intransitive verbs
- If the adjectival part ends in a **consonant** the /ک/ of the auxiliaries drops and become /بدل/ or /ول/

Example: جلا ، سپين

Intransitive	Transitive	Meaning	Adjective	Ending Sound
جلاکبدل to get separated	جلاکول To separate	Separate	جلا	Vowel
سپينبدل to get whitened	سپينول To whiten	White	سپين	Consonant

Exercise:

Intransitive	Transitive	Meaning	Adjective
		empty	خالي
		made	جوړ
		ronconciled	پخلا
		fine	سم
		black	تور
		white	سپين
		broken	خراب
		known	مالوم
		open	ښکاره
		ruined	تباه
		destructed	برباد
		destroyed	ويجاړ
		brush	جارو
		clean	پاک
		separate	جلا

Formation of Tense (merger with *to be*)

(a) Intransitive and (b) Transitive

(a) Intransitive

1) Perfective and 2) Imperfective

1. **Perfective**:
   - The adjectival part of the verb inflects the subject
   - In Present tense the auxiliary verb /کېدل،بدل/ changes into /شـ/ and merges with *be*
   - In Past tense the auxiliary verb /کېدل،بدل/ changes into /شو/ and merges with *be*

Examples: جوړېدل

be + (شو/ or /شـ + *adjective*) verb + subject

Past (شو)	Present (شـ)	Gender	Number	Person
زه جوړ شوم	زه جوړ شم	m	S	
زه جوړه شوم	زه جوړه شم	f		
موږ جوړ شو	موږ جوړه شو	m	P	1
موږ جوړې شوو	موږ جوړې شو	f		
ته جوړ شوې	ته جوړ شې	m	S	
ته جوړه شوې	ته جوړه شې	f		
تاسې جوړ شوئ	تاسې جوړ شئ	m	P	2
تاسې جوړې شوئ	تاسې جوړې شئ	f		
دی جوړ شؤ	دی جوړ شي	m	s	3
دا جوړه شوه	دا جوړه شي	f		
دوی جوړ شول	دوی جوړ شي	m	p	
دوی جوړې شوې	دوی جوړې شي	f		

2. Imperfective:

- In Present tense the auxiliary verb /بدل،کېدل/ changes into / بېږ،کېږ / and merges with *be*
- In Past tense the auxiliary verb /بدل،کېدل/ merges with *be* without any change

be + (کېږ/ بېږ/ بدل/کېدل) + *adjective*) **verb** + **subject**

Past (بدل/کېدل)	Present (بېږ/کېږ)	Gender	Number	Person
زه جوړ بدلېدلم	زه جوړ بېږم	M	S	
زه جوړه بدلېدلم	زه جوړه بېږم	F		
موږ جوړ بدلېدلو	موږ جوړ بېږو	M	P	1
موږ جوړې بدلېدلو	موږ جوړې بېږو	F		
ته جوړ بدلېدلي	ته جوړ بېږې	M	S	
ته جوړه بدلېدلي	ته جوړه بېږې	F		2
تاسې جوړ بدلېدلئ	تاسې جوړ بېږئ	M	P	
تاسې جوړې بدلېدلئ	تاسې جوړې بېږئ	F		
دی جوړ بدلېدلؤ	دی جوړ بېږي	M	s	3
دا جوړه بدلېده	دا جوړه بېږي	F		
دوی جوړ بدلېدل	دوی جوړ شي	M	P	
دوی جوړې بدلېدلې	دوی جوړې شي	F		

(b) Transitive

1) Perfective and 2) Imperfective

1. Perfective:

- In Present tense the auxiliary verb /ول،کول/ changes into /کـ/ and merges with *be,* and verb inflects the **Subject,** however, the adjectival part always inflect the object
- In Past tense the auxiliary verb /ول،کول/ changes into /کړ/ and merges with *be,* and verb inflects the **object**

Examples: جوړول

be + (کړ/ or /کـ + *adjective*) **verb** + **object** + **subject**

37

Past (کړ)	Present (کـ)	Gender	Number	Person
ډاکټر زه موټر جوړ کړم	زه موټر جوړ کم	m	S	
ډاکټر زه لاری جوړه کړم	زه لاری جوړه کم	f		
ډاکټر موږ موټرونه جوړ کړو	موږ موټرونه جوړ کو	m	P	1
ډاکټر موږ لاری جوړي کړو	موږ لاری جوړي کو	f		
ډاکټر ته موټر جوړ کړې	ته موټر جوړ کې	m	S	
ډاکټر ته لاری جوړه کړې	ته لاری جوړه کې	f		
ډاکټر تاسې موټر جوړ کړئ	تاسې موټرونه جوړ کئ	m	P	2
ډاکټر تاسې لاری جوړي کړئ	تاسې لاری جوړي کئ	f		
ډاکټر دی موټر جوړ کؤ/کړؤ	دی موټر جوړ کي	M	s	
ډاکټر دا موټر جوړه کړه	دا لاری جوړه کي	F		
ډاکټر دوی موټر جوړ کړل	دوی موټرونه جوړ کي	M	p	3
ډاکټر دوی موټر جوړي کړي	دوی لاری جوړي کي	F		

2. Imperfective:

- In Present tense only the /ل/ of the auxiliary verb /ول،کول/ drops and merges with *be,* and verb inflects the **Subject**
- In Past tense the auxiliary verb /کول/ no changes and it merges with *be,* and verb inflects the **object**

Examples: جوړول

be + (/ل/ drops in present) **verb** + **object** + **subject**

Past	Present (ل drops)	Gender	Number	Person
ډاکټر زه جوړولم	زه موټر جوړ وم	m	S	
ډاکټرزه جوړولم	زه موټر جوړوم	f		
ډاکټر موږ جوړولو	موږ موټر جوړوو	m	P	1
ډاکټر موږ جوړولو	موږ موټر جوړوو	f		
ډاکټر ته جوړولې	ته موټر جوړوې	m	S	
ډاکټر ته جوړلې	ته موټر جوړوې	f		
ډاکټر تاسې جوړولئ	تاسې موټر جوړوئ	m	P	2
ډاکټر تاسې جوړولئ	تاسې موټر جوړوئ	f		
ډاکټر دی جوړولؤ	دی موټر جوړوي	M	s	
ډاکټر دا جوړوله	دا موټر جوړوي	F		
ډاکټر دوی جوړول	دوی موټر جوړوي	M	p	3
ډاکټر دوی جوړولي	دوی موټر جوړوي	F		

2. _Short_ compound verbs of the auxiliaries /ول/ and /بدل/

- These verbs are somewhat confusing as they have the characteristics of both simple verbs and long compound verbs when used in **perfective** and **imperfective** respectively
- The auxiliary/ول،بدل/ merges so closely with a noun that the **former** generally loses its /ک/ and the **latter** also looses one or two letters. As a result most of the times the noun loses it **meaning, number** and **gender** if separated from the auxiliary.
- In Past perfective the transitive auxiliary /ول/ and the intransitive auxiliary /بدل/ both are **unchangeable**. In other words they do not change into /کړ/ and /شو, /.
- However in present imperfective the intransitive auxiliary /بدل/changes into /یږ/.
- In both Present and Past perfective tense a /و/ is prefixed to it same as in **simple** verbs.

a) Transitive:

Perfective:

Subject	object	/و/	v(ول/و---)	be

Imperfective:

Subject	object		v(ول/و---)	be

b) Intransitive:

Perfective:

Subject	object	/و/	v(بدل/یږ---)	be

Imperfective:

Subject	object		v(بدل/یږ---)	be

Past Imperfective	Past Perfective	Present Imperfective	Present Perfective (_aorist_)	Verb
سپي ښځه وبروله The dog was frightening the woman.	سپي ښځه و بروله A dog frightened the woman	سپی ښځه وبَرَوي A dog frightens/ is frightening the woman	سپی ښځه و وبروي؟ Should the dog frighten the woman?	وبرول to frighten
ښځه وبرېدله The woman was getting frightened.	ښځه و وبرېدله The woman got frightened.	ښځه وبرېږي The woman gets/ is getting frightened.	ښځه و وبربږي؟ Should the woman get frightened?	وبربدل to fear

39

Compound/Simple Verbs in Present and Past Tense

Past		Present		Meanings	Verb
Imperfective	**Perfective**	**Imperfective**	**Perfective**		
I was playing guitar رباب ژغولو Guitar was playing رباب وژغېدلو	ماربا وژغولو رباب وژغېدلو	زه رباب ژغوم رباب ژغېږي	زه رباب و ژغوم رباب و ژغېږي	to play/make sound/speak to be played	ژغول ژغېدل
I was slipping foot ما پښه ښنویوله my foot was slipping زما پښه ښنوبدله	ما و ښنویوله زما پښه وښنوبدله	زه پښه ښنویوم زه وښنوېږم	زه وښنویوم زه وښنوېږم	to make to slip to slip	ښنویول ښنوبدل
I was making you laugh ما ته وخندولې I was laughing زه خندېدلم	ما ته وخندولې زه وخندبدلم	زه تا خندوم زه خندېږم	زه وخندوم زه وخندېږم	to make to laugh to smile	خندول خندبدل
I was making you cry ما ته وژرولې I was crying زه ژړبدلم	ما ته وژړلې زه وژړبدلم	زه تاوژروم زه ژړېږم	زه تاوژروم زه ژړېږم	to make to cry to cry	ژرول ژړبدل
I was falling leaves ما پاڼي رژولې Leaves were falling پاڼي رژېدلې	ماپاڼي ورژولې پاڼي ورژبدلي	زه پاڼي ورژوم پاڼي رژبږي	زه پاڼي ورژوم پاڼي و رژبږي	to fall/drop to fall/drop	رژول رژبدل
I was making car reach ماموټر ورسولو The car was reaching موټر رسېدلو	ماموټر وررسولو موټر ورسبدلو	زه موټررسوم موټررسبږي	زه موټرورسوم زه ورسبږم	To make reach/ deliver To reach	رسول رسبدل
I was smiling زه مسېدلم	زه ومسبدلم	زه مسېږم	زه و مسبږم	To make smile To smile	مسول مسبدل
Book was falling کتاب له مېزه لوېدلی from the table	کتاب له مېزه ولوبدلی	کتاب له مېزه لوبږي	کتاب له مېزه ولوبږي	To drop/fall	لوبدل
I was causing the girl dance ما نجلۍ نخوله Girl was dancing نجلۍ نخبدله	ما نجلۍ ونخوله نجلۍ ونخبدله	زه نجلۍ نخوم نجلۍ ونخبږي	زه نجلۍ ونخوم نجلۍ ونخبږي	To make to dance To dance	نخول نخبدل
Driver was deceiving the police موټروان پولیس غولولو Man was erring سړی غولبدلو	موټروان پولیس وغولولو سړی وغولبدلو	موټروان پولیس غولوي سړی غولبږي	موټروان پولیس وغولوي سړی وغولبږي	To deceive To get deceive/ to err	غولول غولبدل
Dog was frightening the man سپي سړی وډبرولو Man was fearing سړی وډبربدلو	سپي سړی وډبرولو سړی وډبربدلو	سپی سړی وډبروي	سپی سړی و ډبروي سړی و ډبربږي	To frighten To fear	ډبرول ډبربدل
I was searching book ما کتاب لټولو I was searching زه په کتاب پسي لټبدلم	ما کتاب ولټولو زه په کتاب پسي ولټبدلم	زه کتاب لټوم زه په کتاب پسي لټبږم	زه کتاب ولټوم زه په کتاب پسي ولټبږم	To search To search	لټول لټبدل
Mother was washing the kid مورماشوم لمبولو Kid was taking bath ماشوم لمببدلو	مورماشوم ولمبولو ماشوم ولومببدلو	مورماشوم ولمبوي ماشوم لومببږي	مورماشوم ولمبوي ماشوم ولومببږي	To wash To take bath	لمبول لمببدل
Police was pacifying the boys پولیس هلکان ګواښبول Father was warning the son پلار زوی ته ګواښبدلو	پلار زوی ته وګواښبدلو	پلار زوی ته ګواښبږي	پلار زوی ته و ګواښبږي	To separate/pacify To warn/threaten	ګواښبول ګواښبدل
I was compelling the dog to bear ما سپي صبرولو the dog was bearing سپي وصبربدلو	ما سپي وصبرولو سپي وصبربدلو	زه سپي صبروم سپي صبربږي	زه سپي وصبروم سپي و صبربږي	To make to endure/bear To patience	صبرول صبربدل
Jet was raining bombs الوتکي بمونه ورول Rain was raining باران ورېدلو	الوتکي بمونه و ورول باران و ورېدلو	الوتکه بمونه وروي باران ورېږي	الوتکه بمونه و روي باران و ورېږي	To rain/ shower To rain	ورول ورېدل
State was making the troops fight دولت عسکر جنګول Troops were fighting عسکر جنګېدل	دولت عسکروجنګول عسکر وجنګېدل	دولت عسکرجنګوي عسکر جنګبږي	دولت عسکر و جنګوي عسکر و جنګبږي	To make to fight To fight	جنګول جنګبدل
He was causing the parrot هلک توتي چغول	هلک توتي	هلک توتي چغوي	هلک توتي وچغوي	To make ---	چغول

40

English				English meaning	Pashto
scream توتي چغېدلو Parrot was screaming	وچغولو توتي و چغېدلو	توتي چغېږي	توتي و چغېږي	sound/cry/shout To sound	چغېدل
I was delaying the work ما كار خنډولو I was delaying زه خنډېدلم	ما كار وخنډولو زه وخنډېدلم	زه كار خنډوم زه خنډېږم	زه كار وخنډوم زه وخنډېږم	To suspend/delay To delay	خنډول خنډېدل
Soldier was torturing the عسكر بندي خورولو prisoner the prisoner was getting torture بندي خورېدلو	عسكر بندي و خورولو بندي و خورېدلو	عسكر بندي خوروي بندي خورېږي	عسكر بندي و خوروي بندي و خورېږي	To torture To get torture	خورول خورېدل
I was dripping water ما اوبه څڅولي water was dripping اوبه څڅېدلي	ما اوبه وڅڅولي اوبه وڅڅېدلي	زه اوبه څڅوم اوبه څڅېږي	زه اوبه وڅڅوم اوبه وڅڅېږي	To drip To drip	څڅول څڅېدل
I was tearing paper ما كاغذ شلولو Paper was tearing كاغذ شلېدلو	ما كاغذ وشلولو كاغذ و شلېدلو	زه كاغذ شلوم كاغذ شلېږي	زه كاغذ وشلوم كاغذ و شلېږي	To tear To get tear	شلول شلېدل
I was destroying the wall ما دېوال نړولو Wall was falling دېوال نړېدلو	ما دېوال و نړولو دېوال و نړېدلو	زه دېوال نړوم دېوال و نړېږي	زه دېوال و نړوم دېوال و نړېږي	To destroy/ fall To destroy/fall	نړول نړېدل
I was stretching the foot ما پښه غځوله I was stretching زه غځېدلم	ما پښه وغځوله زه و غځېدلم	زه پښه غځوم زه غځېږم	زه پښه وغځوم زه و غځېږم	To stretch To get stretch	غځول غځېدل
Fever was shivering me تبې زه لړزولم I was shivering زه لړزېدلم	تبې زه ولړزولم زه و لړزېدلم	تبه مالړزوي زه لړزېږم	تبه ما ولړزوي زه و لړزېږم	To make shiver To get shiver	لړزول لړزېدل
I was flowing water ما اوبه بهولي Water was flowing اوبه بهېدلي	ما اوبه و بهولي اوبه و بهېدلي	زه اوبه بهوم اوبه بهېږي	زه اوبه و بهوم اوبه و بهېږي	To make flow To flow	بهول بهېدل
					څینځول څینځېدل
I was moving the car ما موټر چلولو The car was moving موټر چلېدلو	ما موټر و چلولو موټر و چلېدلو	زه موټر چلوم موټر چلېږي	زه موټر و چلوم موټر و چلېږي	To run /move To get run/move	چلول چلېدل
				To contaminate To get contaminate	شرول شرېدل
I was frightening the dog ما سپی ترهولو The dog was fearing سپی ترهېدلو	ما سپی و ترهولو سپی و ترهېدلو	زه سپی ترهوم سپی ترهېږي	زه سپی و ترهوم سپی و ترهېږي	To frighten To fear	ترهول ترهېدل
Husband was disgracing the مېړه ښځه شرموله lady The lady was getting shy ښځه شرمېدله	مېړه ښځه و شرموله ښځه و شرمېدله	مېړه ښځه شرموي ښځه شرمېږي	مېړه ښځه و شرموي ښځه و شرمېږي	To disgrace To get sham/shy	شرمول شرمېدل
I was unfolding the shawl ما څادر غورولو The flower was گل غورېدلو unfolding/blooming	ما څادر و غورولو گل و غورېدلو	زه څادر غورم گل غورېږي	زه څادر و غورم گل و غورېږي	To make unfold To get unfold	غورول غورېدل
I was constructing the house ما كور رغولو the house was getting construct كور رغېدلو	ما كور و رغولو كور و رغېدلو	زه كور رغوم كور رغېږي	زه كور و رغوم كور و رغېږي	To construct/ make healthy To get constructed/ to become healthy	رغول رغېدل
I was painting the house ما كور رنگولو the house was getting paint كور رنگېدلي	ما كور و رنگولو كور و رنگېدلي	زه كور رنگوم كور رنگېږي	زه كور و رنگوم كور و رنگېږي	To paint To get paint	رنگول رنگېدل
I was billing the water ما اوبه خوټولي Water was boiling اوبه و خوټېدلي	ما اوبه و خوټولي اوبه و خوټېدلي	زه اوبه خوټوم اوبه و خوټېږي	زه اوبه و خوټوم اوبه و خوټېږي	To boil To get boil	خوټول خوټېدل
Girl was jingling bangles نجلي بنگړي شرنگول Bangles were jingling بنگړي شرنگېدل				To jingle To get jingle	شرنگول شرنگېدل
He was provoking you. هغه ته ولمسولي You were getting provoke ته لمسېدلي	هغه ته ولمسولي ته و لمسېدلي	هغه تا لمسوم ته لمسېږي	هغه تا ولمسوم ته و لمسېږي	To provoke To get provoke	لمسول لمسېدل
We were thwarting the enemy موږ دوښمن تمبولو the enemy was getting thwart دوښمن تمبېدلو	موږ دوښمن و تمبولو دوښمن و تمبېدلو	موږ دوښمن تمبوو دوښمن و تمبېږي	موږ دوښمن و تمبوو دوښمن و تمبېږي	To thwart To get thwart	تمبول تمبېدل

41

I was causing the loin roar موږزمری غورمبولؤ Loin was roaring زمری غورمبیدلؤ	موږزمری و غورمبولؤ زمری وغورمبیدلؤ	موږزمری غورمبوو زمری غورمبیبږي	زه زمری وغورمبوم زمری وغورمبېږي	To make roar To get roar	غورمبول غورمبیدل
I was knocking the door ما ورتکولؤ Door was getting knock ورتکبدلؤ	ما ورتکولؤ ورتکبدلؤ	زه ورتکوم ورتکبږي	زه ورتکوم ورتکبږي	To beat/knock To get beat/knock	تکول تکبدل
I was knocking the door ما درازه وډبوله The door was getting knock دروازه ډبیدله	ما دروازه وډبوله دروازه وډبیدله	زه دروازه وډبوم دروازه ډببږي	زه دروازه وډبوم دروازه ډببږي	To beat/knock To get beat/knock	ډبول ډبیدل
I was causing the horse gallop ما اسپه ترپوله the hors was galloping اسپه ترپبدله	ما اسپه ترپوم اسپه وترپبدله	زه اسپه وترپوم اسپه ترپبږي/ ترپي	زه اسپه وترپوم اسپه وترپبږي/ وترپي	To cause to gallop To gallop	ترپول ترپبدل
				To make sparkle/glitter To sparkle/glitter	ځرکول ځرکبدل
I was making you turn ما ته گرځولمې You were turning ته گرځېدلې	ما ته وگرځولمې ته وگرځېدلې	زه تا وگرځوم ته وگرځبږي/ وگرځي	زه تا وگرځوم ته وگرځبږي/ گرځي	To make walk/turn To walk/ turn	گرځول گرځبدل
I was moving you ما ته وښنورلمې You were moving ته وښنورېدلې	ما ته وښنورلمې ته وښنورېدلې	زه تا وښنورم ته وښنوربږي/ ښنوري	زه تا وښنورم ته وښنوري	To make move To move	ښنورول ښنورېدل
I was spending the money ما پیسې لگولې Money was getting spend پیسې لگېدلې	ما پیسې ولگولې پیسې ولگبدلې	زه پیسې ولگوم پیسې ولگبږي/ لگي	زه پیسې ولگوم پیسې ولگبږي/ ولگي	To set/put into action To get into action	لگول لگبدل
I was throwing the stone ما ډبره وغورځوله Stone was getting throw زه غورځبدلم	ما ډبره وغورځوله زه وغورځبدلم	زه ډبره وغورځوم زه وغورځبږم/ غورځم	زه ډبره وغورځوم زه وغورځبږم/ وغورځم	To throw To get throw	غورځول غورځبدل
I was moving you ما ته وخوځولمې You were moving زه خوځبدلم	ما ته وخوځولمې زه وخوځبدلم	زه تا وخوځوم زه خوځبږم/ خوځم	زه تا وخوځوم زه وخوځبږم/ وخوځم	To make move To get move	خوځول خوځبدل
I was rotating you ما ته ځرخولمې You were rotating زه ځرخبدلم	ما ته وځرخولمې زه وځرخبدلم	زه تا ځرخوم زه ځرخبږم/ ځرخم	زه تا وځرخوم زه وځرخبږم/ وځرخم	To make turn/rotate To get turn/rotate	ځرخول ځرخبدل
I was making you run ما ته وځغلولې I was running زه وځغلبدلم	ما ته وځغلولې زه وځغلبدلم	زه تا وځغلوم زه وځغلم	زه تا وځغلوم زه وځغلبږم/زه وځغلم	To make --- run To run	ځغلول ځغلبدل
I was making you flee ما ته وتښتولمې You were fleeing زه تښتبدلم	ما ته وتښتولمې زه وتښتبدلم	زه تا وتښتوم زه وتښتبږم/زه تښتم	زه تا وتښتوم زه وتښتبږم/وتښتم	To make---flee To flee	تښتول تښتبدل
I was waving the flag ما بیرغ ورپولؤ the flag was waving بیرغ ورپبدلؤ	ما بیرغ ورپولؤ بیرغ ورپبدلؤ	زه بیرغ ورپوم بیرغ ورپبږي/ بیرغ رپي	زه بیرغ ورپوم بیرغ ورپبږي/ بیرغ ورپي	To wave To get wave	رپول رپبدل
I was boiling the tea ما چای واېشولؤ the tea was boiling لاوه اېشبدله	ما چای واېشولؤ لاوه واېشبدله	زه چای واېشوم لاوه واېشبږي/لاوه اېشي	زه چای واېشوم لاوه واېشبږي/لاوه واېشي	To make boil To get boil	اېشول اېشبدل
Woman was giving birth the boy ښنځي هلک زبروولؤ The boy was b هلک زبربدلؤ	ښنځي هلک وزبروولؤ هلک وزبربدلؤ	ښنځه هلک زبروي هلک زبري	ښنځه هلک وزبروي هلک وزبري	To give birth To be born	زبرول زبربدل
I was shining my self ما ځان ځلولؤ I was shining زه ځلبدلم	ما ځان وځلولؤ زه وځلبدلم	زه ځان وځلوم زه ځلبږم/ زه ځلم	زه ځان وځلوم زه وځلبږم/ زه وځلم	To make shine To get shine	ځلول ځلبدل
I was making the animals graze ما څاروي وڅرول Animals were grazing څاروي څربدل	ما څاروي وڅرول څاروي وڅربدل	زه څاروي وڅروم څاروي څربږي/ څاروي څري	زه څاروي وڅروم څاروي وڅربږي/څاروي وڅري	To make graze Go graze	څرول څربدل
I was stopping you ما ته ودرولمې You were stopping ته درېدلې	ما ته ودرولمې ته ودرېدلې	زه تا دروم ته درپږي/ته دري	زه تا ودروم ته ودرپږي/ته ودري	To make stop/stand To stop/stand	درول درېدل

42

I was rolling the stone ما کانی رغرولو The stone was rolling کانی رغبدلو	ما کانی ورغرولو کانی ورغبدلو	زه کانی رغروم کانی رغبپي کانی رغري	زه کانی ورغروم کانی ورغبپي کانی ورغري	To make roll To get role	رغرول رغبدل
I was dripping the water ما اوبه څخولي The water was dripping اوبه څڅبدلي	ما اوبه وڅخولي اوبه وڅڅبدلي	زه اوبه څخوم اوبه څڅبپي/اوبه څاڅي	زه اوبه وڅخوم اوبه وڅڅبپي/اوبه وڅاڅي	To make drip To get drip	څخول څڅبدل
Police was making the thief run پولیس غل څخغلولو Thief was running غل څخغلبدلو	پولیس غل وڅخغلولو غل وڅخغلبدلو	پولیس غل څخغلوي غل څخغلبپي/غل وڅغلي	پولیس غل وڅخغلوي غل وڅخغلبپي/غل وڅغلي	To make run To run	څخغلول څخغلبدل

Compound verbs of shifting stress

- These compound verbs have **other** auxiliaries than /کول/ and /کېدل/, such as وتل، وهل، ناستل and others

- The auxiliaries are suffixed generally to adjectives

- In these verbs no major change happens except **shifting of the stress** from first part to second part of the verb in perfective and imperfective positions respectively.

(Past and Present Tense)

a) **Perfective:**
The stress occurs on the **first** part (adjective) of the verb

b) **Imperfective:**
The stress shifts to the **second** part (auxiliary) of the verb.

Past Imperfective	Past Perfective	Present Imperfective	Present Perfective (*aorist*)	Verb
ما دروازه پوري وهله I was pushing the door.	ما دروازه پوري وهله I pushed the door.	زه دروازه پوري وهم I push / am pushing the door.	زه دروازه پوري وهم May I push the door	پوري وهل to push
زه کښېناستلم I was sitting down.	زه کښېناستلم I sat down.	زه کښېنم I sit / am sitting down.	زه کښېنم May I sit down	کښېناستل to sit down

43

Compound Verbs of the Shifting Stress (*Intransitive*)

Past			Present			Meanings	Verb
Imperfective	*Perfective*	Subject	*Imperfective*	*Perfective*	Subject		*All irregular*
کښېناستلم	کښېناستلم	زه موږ ته تاسې دی دوی د/ دوی	کښېنم	کښېنم	زه موږ ته تاسې دی دوی د/ دوی	to sit	کښېناستل
						to be traped	کښېناوتل
						to lie down	څملاستل
						to be deceived	خطاوتل
						to cross over	پوري وتل
						to go under	لاندې وتل
						to return	جاروتل
						to enter	ننه وتل
						to lie down	پري وتل

Compound Verbs of the Shifting Stress (*Transitive*)

Past				Present			Meanings	Verb
Imperfective	*Perfective*	Obj	Subj	*Imperfective*	*Perfective*	Subject		*All irregular except the first three*
		زه موږ ته تاسې دی دوی د/ دوی	ما موږ تا دې ده دوی			زه موږ ته تاسې دی دوی د/ دوی	to make sit	کښېنول
							to make lay	څملول
							to push	پوري وهل
							to put down	کښې بنودل
							to leave	پري بنودل
							to trap	کښې ايستل
							to make cross	پوري ايستل
							to insert under	لاندې ايستل
							to make return	جار ايستل
							to enter/insert	ننه ايستل
							to lay down	پري ايستل
							to open	پرا نيستل
							to take/drive	بوتلل
							to bring back	راوستل
							to bring/ fetch	راوړل

44

Irregular verbs

- Generally Pashto verbs are irregular only in **present** and **future** tense

- Only verbs کېدل، کول ، ورتلل ، در ، را ، تلل، مرل، اېښنودل، ورل are irregular also in past perfective

- There is no irregular verb in **past imperfective** tense

Past		Present		Meanings	Verb
Imperfective	Perfective	Imperfective	Perfective		
(1) In present imperfective tense the infinitive /تلل/ changes into /خـ/, while in present and past perfective tense it changes respectively into /ولاړ/ and /ولاړش/ Verbs/ورتلل،در،را/ in Present perfective change into /ورش،در،را/ while in Past perfective they change into /ورغل،در،را/					
تلل	ولاړ	خـ	ولاړش	to go	تلل
راتلل	راغل	راخـ	راش	to come towards the 1st person / spot	راتلل
ورتلل	ورغل	ورخـ	ورش	to come/go to the 3rd person/spot	ورتلل
درتلل	درغل	درخـ	درش	to come towards the 2nd person / spot	درتلل
بوتلل	بوتلل	بوخـ	بوخـ	to drive/ take/ guide animate/ moving things	بوتلل
(2) /وتل/ is replaced by /خـ/.					
وتل	وَتل	وخـ	وَوخـ	to exit/ get out	وتل
ننوتل	ننوتل	ننوخـ	ننوخـ	to get in/ enter	ننوتل
الوتل	وَالوتل	الوخـ	وَالوخـ	to fly	الوتل
جاروتل	جاروتل	جاروخـ	جاروخـ	to return/ surround	جاروتل
کنبوتل	کنبوتل	کنبوخـ	کنبوخـ	to get stuck in/ traped	کنبوتل
پوریوتل	پوریوتل	پوریوخـ	پوریوخـ	to cross over	پوریوتل
لاندیوتل	لاندیوتل	لاندیوخـ	لاندیوخـ	to go underneath	لاندیوتل
تېروتل	تېروتل	تېروخـ	تېروخـ	to miss/ make a mistake	تېروتل
خطاوتل	خطاوتل	خطاوخـ	خطاوخـ	to miss/ make a	خطاوتل

				mistake	
پرېوتل	پرېوتل	پرېوځ	پرېوځ	to lie down/ fall	پرېوتل
ترغاړپوتل	ترغاړپوتل	ترغاړپوځ	ترغاړپوځ	to hug	ترغاړپوتل

(3) The infinitive of /ايستل/ /باس/ changes into

ايستل	وَ ايستل	باس	وَ باس	to expel/ put off	ايستل
کنبي ايستل	کنبي ايستل	کنبي باس	کنبي باس	to trap	کنبي ايستل
تېرايستل	تېرايستل	تېرباس	تېرباس	to deceive	تېرايستل
خطا ايستل	خطا ايستل	خطا باس	خطا باس	to deceive	خطا ايستل
پرې اسيتل	پرې اسيتل	پرې باس	پرې باس	to stretch/ lie down	پرې اسيتل
لاندي ابستل	لاندي ابستل	لاندي باس	لاندي باس	to make cross underneath	لاندي ابستل
ننه ايستل	ننه ايستل	ننه باس	ننه باس	to enter	ننه ايستل
اړ ايستل	اړ ايستل	اړ باس	اړ باس	to force/ compel	اړ ايستل

(4) Those verbs which end in /ستل/ the letter of /ست/ are dropped and only the letter /ـل/remains;

However, the verb /اغوستل/changes into /اغوند/ and /پرانيستل/ changes into /پرانيز/

راوستل	راوستل	راول	راول	to bring (animate or moving things like cars)	راوستل
دروستل	دروستل	درول	درول		دروستل
وروستل	وروستل	ورول	ورول		وروستل
اخيستل	وَاخيستل	اخل	وَاخل	to take/buy	اخيستل
خُغستل	وَخُغستل	خُغل	وَخُغل	to run	خُغستل
لوستل	وَلوستل	لول	وَ لول	to read / study	لوستل
پرانيستل	پرانيستل	پرانيز	پرانيز	to open/ inaugurate	پرانيستل
اغوستل	وَ اغوستل	اغوند	واغوند	to wear/ put on	اغوستل

(5) In the verbs /استل/ /خملاستل/ and /کنبناستل/ the last four letters /استل/ are dropped.

کنبناستل	کنبناستل	کنبن	کنبن	to sit down	کنبناستل
خملاستل	خملاستل	خمل	خمل	to lie down/ stretch away	خملاستل

(6) In verb /ويشتل/ the /يشت/ drops in present imperfective, while in present perfective only /شت/ drops

ويشتل	وَ ويشتل	ول	وَويل	to shoot/ hit	ويشتل

46

(7) In the verbs نتل/ښتل اوښتل، رغبښتل،نغوښتل،غوښتل، را غوښتل the last /نتل/ changes into /ار/ or /ار/

غوښتل	وَ غوښتل	غوارِ	وَغوارِ	to want/ like/ demand	غوښتل
نغښتل	وَ نغښتل	نغارِ	وَنغارِ	to cover/ wrap	نغښتل
اوښتل	وَ اوښتل	اورِ	وَاورِ	To cross over	اوښتل
رغښتل	وَ رغښتل	رغِي	وَ رغِي	To rol over	رغبښتل

(8) In the verbs کښل/ and را کښل/ the final /ښل/ changes into /ار/

کښل	وَ کښل	کارِ	وَ کارِ	to draw	کښل
را کښل	را وَ کښل	راکارِ	را وَکارِ	to pull	را کښل
کښې کښل	کښې کښل	کښې کارِ	کښې کارِ	to push/ press	کښې کښل

(9) In the verbs ښودل/ پرې ښودل/ and کښې ښودل/ the last /ښد/ changes into /بد/

پرې ښودل	پرې ښودل	پربِد	پربِد	to leave	پرې ښودل
کښې ښودل	کښې ښودل	کښبِد	کښبِد	to put/ keep	کښې ښودل

(10) In verbs خوړل/ the sound of /ر/ changes into /ر/

خوړل	خوړل	خور	وَ خور	to eat	خوړل
مړکبدل	مړش	مر	وَ مر	to die	مرل

(11) In the verbs of وول/پیوول/ and بیوول/ the "وول" is replaced by "اي".

پژول	وَ پژول	پیاي	وَ پیاي	to heard	پژول
بژول	وَ بژول	بیاي	وَ بیاي	to take/ drive/ guide (animate or moving objects)	بژول

(12) In the verbs دل/ اوبدل/ and پیژندل/ the letters of /د/ is dropped.

پیژندل	وَ پیژندل	پیژن	وَ پیژن	to know	پیژندل
اوبدل	وَ اوبدل	اوب	وَ اوب	to weave / knit	اوبدل

(13) In verb وژل/ the final /ل/ is replaced by /ن/.

وژل	وَ وژل	وژن	وَ وژن	to kill	وژل

(14) In the verb موندل/ the /ندل/ is replaced by /م/.

موندل	وَ موندل	موم/ موند	وَ موم/وَ موند	to find	موندل

(15) In verb نښتل/ the letter of /ت/ is dropped

نښتل	وَ نښتل	نښل	وَ نښل	to stick/ touch/ to get stuck in	نښتل

		(16) The verb /ختل/ changes into /خېژ/.			
ختـﻟ	وَ ختـﻟ	خېژ	وَ خېژ	to climb/ rise/ come out	ختل
		(17) The verb /کتل/ changes into /ګور/ and /لیدل/ changes into /وینـ/			
کتـﻟ	وَ کتـﻟ	ګور	وَ ګور	to look/ watch	کتل
لیدـﻟ	وَ لیدـﻟ	وینـ	وَ وینـ	to see	لیدل
		(18) The verb /وړل/ in both present and past perfective یۀ is added before the verb and in the latter also (to be +سـ) at the end of the verb			
وړـﻟ	یۀوړـﻟ	وړ	یۀسـ	to take	وړل
		(19) In the verb /بلل/ a /وَ/ is added in the middle			
بلـﻟ	وَ بلـﻟ	بول	وَ بوَل	to call/ consider/ sing	بلل
		(20) In present tense the verb /ښنودل/ښوول/ is replaced by equivalent /ښنیل/.			
ښنود	وَ ښنود	ښنیـ	وَ ښنیـ	to show/ teach	ښنودل/ښوول ښنیل
		(21) The verb /اېښنودل/ changes into /ږد/ only in Present imperfective			
اېښنودـﻟ	کېنـﭑښنودـﻟ	ږد	کېنـﭑږد	to keep/ put	اېښنودل
		(22) The verb /کېدل/ in Present perfect changes into /شـ/ and imperfective into /کېږ/ while in Past perfective it changes into /شو/			
کېدـﻟ	وَ شوَ	کېږ	وَ شـ	to be	کېدل
		(23) The verb /کول/ only as an auxiliary is irregular. In Present perfective changes into /کـ/ while in Past perfective it changes into /کړ/			
پوخلا کول	پوخلا کړِ	پوخلا کوَ	پوخلا کـ	to reconcile	پوخلا کول
		(24) In the following verbs the infinitive (ل) is dropped and an (ا) is added after the first letter: (خندل، ژړل، غپل، ویل)			
خندل/ژړل/غپل/ویل	وَ خندل/ژړل/غپل/ویل	خاند/ژاړ/ غاپ/وایـ	وَ خاند/ژاړ/غاپ/وایـ غاپ/وایـ		

Also note the following irregular verbs:

اخښنل=اغږل، پېرودل=پېرل، چاودل/چول، رودل=رول، سوزېدل=سول، موښنل=مښل،

Objectless Transitive Verbs in the **Past** tense

1. These verbs look like intransitive verbs but in fact they are **transitive**
2. They do not have an independent **object**, rather they are used **themselves** as objects
3. They always take the ending of 3rd person masculine in past tenses
4. Their subject is always put into the **agentive** case
5. Generally these verbs are associated with **physical** actions of humans and animals
6. Most of them also have **intransitive** version as well
7. In **Present** tense they do not pose any confusion because it the **subject** which inflects, not the object

Use in Past Tense	Intransitive version	Use in Past tense	Meaning	Transitive version
زه و پرنجېدلم	پرنجېدل	ما و پرنجل	to sneeze	پرنجل
ته و ټوخېدلې	ټوخېدل	تا و ټوخل	to cough	ټوخل
دی و خندېدلؤ	خندېدل	ده و خندل	to laugh	خندل
دا و ژړېدله	ژړېدل	دې و ژړل	to cry	ژړل
زه و لمبېدلم	لمبېدل	ما و لامبل	to take a bath	لامبل
سپې و غپېدلؤ	غپېدل	سپي و غپل	to bark	غپل
سپې وَ غیرژپېدلؤ	غیرژپېدل	سپي وَ غیرژل	to roar	غیرژل
خر وَ اونګپېدلؤ	اونګپېدل	خرۀ وَ اونګل		اونګل
سپې و څغلپېدلؤ	څغلپېدل	سپي و څغاستل	to run	څغاستل
اسونه و ترپپېدل	ترپپېدل	اسونو و ترپل	to gallop	ترپل
نجونې و زنګپېدلې	زنګپېدل	نجونو و زانګل	to swing	زانګل
		سترګو وَ څمبل	to blink	څمبل
		غله و دانګل	to run	دانګل
		سړي و توکل	to spit	توکل
		اوبښ وَ میتل	to urinate	میتل
		اس وَ مهزل	to urinate	مهزل
		سړی وَ خړل	to extricate	خړل

49

The verbs of qualitative variability:

1. These **intransitive** verbs indicate *__alteration__* of a particular state
2. The subject pronoun remains in obscurity; that is why the *to be* agrees with the gender and number of the **nominal** part of these verbs which plays the role of a subject
3. In perfective sentences, they don't take / وَ /

Subjective	Qualitative alteration	Meaning	Verb
تیاره وَ شوه	تیاره شوه	darkness	تیاره
رڼا وَ شوه	رڼا شوه	light	رڼا
روژه وَ شوه	روژه شوه	Ramadan	روژه
اختر وَ شؤ	اختر شؤ	Eid	اختر
د هغوی نېکي وَ شوه	د هغوی نېکي شوه	good	نېکي
د هغوی بدي وَ شوه	د هغوی بدي شوه	vice	بدي
زمورږ سره دوښمني وَ شوه	زمورږ سره دوښمني شوه	enmity	دوښمني
زمورږ سره دوستي وَ شوه	زمورږ سره دوستي شوه	friendship	دوستي
ستاسي سره ملگرتیا وَ شوه	ستاسي سره ملگرتیا شوه	friendship	ملگرتیا
د دوی سره جنګ وَ شؤ	د دوی سره جنګ شؤ	war	جنګ
		earthquake	زلزله
زمورږ سره ورؤري وَ شوه	زمورږ سره ورؤري شوه	brotherhood	ورؤري
زمورږ سره یاري وَ شوه	زمورږ سره یاري شوه	friendship	یاري
سره اشنایي مو وَ شوه	سره اشنایي مو شوه	friendship	اشنایي
په مورږ ماتم وَ شؤ	په مورږ ماتم شؤ	mourning	ماتم
په هیواد کښي امن وَ شؤ	په هیواد کښي امن شؤ	peace	امن
اوس سوکالي وَ شوه	اوس سوکالي شوه	prosperity	سوکالي
کراري وَ شوه	کراري شوه	stability	کراري
ارامي وَ شوه	ارامي شوه	tranquillity	ارامي
چوپتیا وَ شوه	چوپتیا شوه	silence	چوپتیا
شور وَ شؤ	شور شؤ	noise	شؤر
زما تبه وَ شؤ	زما تبه شوه	fever	تبه
په سرمي درد وَ شؤ	په سرمي درد شؤ	pain	درد
زګروی مي وَ شؤ	زګروی مي شؤ	groaning	زګروی
ځانکدن یې وَ شؤ	ځانکدن یې شؤ	death throes	ځانکدن
په کور کښي خوشالي وَ شوه	په کور کښي خوشالي شوه	happiness	خوشالي
بنادي وَ شوه	بنادي شوه	prosperity	بنادي
نېکمرغي وَ شوه	نېکمرغي شوه	goodluck	نېکمرغي
خواري وَ شوه	خواري شوه	poverty	خواري
ابادي وَ شوه	ابادي شوه	prosperity	ابادي
وچکالي وَ شوه	وچکالي شوه	drought	وچکالي
باچاهي وَ شوه	باچاهي شوه	kingdom	باچاهي
سکاوي وَ شوه	سکاوي شوه	the rule Sakau	سکاوي

باچاګردي وَ شوه	باچاګردي شوه	anarchy	باچاګردي
انارشي وَ شوه	انارشي شوه	anarchy	انارشي
انقلاب وَ شؤ	انقلاب شؤ	revolution	انقلاب
ګډوډي وَ شوه	ګډوډي شوه	disorder	ګډوډي
هله ګوله وَ شوه	هله ګوله شوه	noise	هله ګوله
لګه درګه وَ شوه	لګه درګه شوه	roit	لګه درګه
ټپل ماټپل وَ شؤ	ټپل ماټپل شؤ	stampede	ټپل ماټپل
غال مغال وَ شؤ	غال مغال شؤ	argument	غال مغال
کش مَکش وَ شؤ	کش مَکش شؤ	contest	کش مَکش
شؤر ماشؤر وَ شؤ	شؤر ماشؤر شؤ	noisc	شور ماشور
ناري، سوري، چيغپ، بوغى وَ شوپ	ناري، سوري، چيغپ، بوغى شوپ	hue and cry	ناري، سوري، چيغپ، بوغى،
ولسواکي وَ شوه	ولسواکي شوه	democracy	ولسواکي
شاهي وَ شوه	شاهي شوه	monarchy	شاهي
ظاهر شاهي وَ شوه	ظاهر شاهي شوه	the rule of King Zahirshah	ظاهرشاهي
ازادي وَ شوه	ازادي شوه	liberty	ازادي
مارشل لا وَ شوه	مارشل لا شوه	Martiallaw	مارشل لا
ديکتاتوري وَ شوه	ديکتاتوري شوه	dictatorship	ديکتاتوري
خپلواکي وَ شوه	خپلواکي شوه	independence	خپلواکي
بوی وَ شؤ	بوی شؤ	smell	بوی
لوګی وَ شؤ	لوګی شؤ	smoke	لوګی
ډډوزه وَ شوه	ډډوزه شوه	smell	ډډوزه
لمبه وَ شوه	لمبه شوه	flame	لمبه
بغ وَ شؤ	بغ شؤ	sound	بغ
ژوب وَ شؤ	ژوب شؤ	noise	ژوب
شؤور وَ شؤ	شؤور شؤ	noise	شور
غلبله وَ شوه	غلبله شوه	roaring	غلبله
ګنګوسې وَ شوپ	ګنګوسې شوپ	rumour	ګنګوسې
اوازه وَ شوه	اوازه شوه	rumour	اوازه
ازانګه وَ شوه	ازانګه شوه	echoe	ازانګه
وړانګه وَ شوه	وړانګه شوه	ray	وړانګه
درزا وَ شوه	درزا شوه	throbbing	درزا
درزهار وَ شؤ	درزهار شؤ	throbbing	درزهار
خندا وَ شوه	خندا شوه	laughter	خندا
ژړا وَ شوه	ژړا شوه	weaping	ژړا
شمښت وَ شؤ	شمښت شؤ	noise	سمښت
غپا وَ شوه	غپا شوه	barking	غپا

51

شخه وَ شوه	شخه شوه	brawl	شخه
دعوه وَ شوه	دعوه شوه	argument	دعوه
مرئه وَ شوه	مرئه شوه	dispute	مرئه
مقابله وَ شوه	مقابله شوه	competition	مقابله
سيالي وَ شوه	سيالي شوه	contest	سيالي
خرخبئ وَ شوي	خرخبئ شوي	brawl	خرخبئ
غوتئ وَ شوه	غوتئ شوه	brawl	غوتئ
موتئ وَ شوي	موتئ شوي	brawl	موتئ
خپرئ وَ شوي	خپرئ شوي	buffet	خپرئ
بحث وَ شؤ	بحث شؤ	discussion	بحث
رینبتینئ وَ شوي	رینبتینئ شوي	argument	رینبتنئ
سپیناوي وَ شؤ	سپیناوي شؤ	argument	سپیناوی
شمال، باد ،بخ، باران، سوری، لمر، سپوږمی، تروږمی، لړه، خوپ وَ شؤ	شمال، باد ،بخ، باران، سوری، لمر، سپوږمی، تروږمی، لړه، خوپ شؤ	wind, wind, clouds, rain, shadow, sun, moon, darknight, fog, smog	شمال، باد ، وریغ، باران، سوری، لمر، سپوږمی/ تروږمی، لړه، خوپ
ژمی،دوبی، منی، سوړمنی، دوبی وَ شؤ	ژمی،دوبی، منی، سوړمنی، دوبی شؤ	winter, autumn, spring, summer	ژمی، منی،سوړمن ی، پسرلی، دوبی
یخ شؤ ، گرمي وَ شوه	یخ شؤ ، گرمي شوه	cold, hot	یخ، گرمي
تالنده وَ شوه	تالنده شوه	thundering	تالنده
تنا وَ شوه	تنا شوه	thundering	تنا
ورځ، شپه، سبا وَ شوه، سهار، گهیځ، ماځیگر، مابنام، ماخوستن وَ شؤ، غرمه وَ شوه، یوه بجه وَ شوه درې بجې وَ شوي	ورځ، شپه، سبا شوه، سهار، گهیځ، ماځیگر، مابنام، ماخوستن شؤ، غرمه شوه، یوه بجه شوه درې بجې شوي	clouds, late, nihgt, morning, evening, one O'colock ...	ورځ، ناوختي، شپه، سبا، سهار، گهیځ، ماځیگر،....، یوه بج، درې بجې
په ښار کښي مي گوزاره وَ شوه	په ښار کښي مي گوزاره شوه	subsistence	گوزاره
ژوند مي په کلي کښي وَ شؤ	ژوند مي په کلي کښي شؤ	life	ژوند

52

Genitive Verbs of emotion

- The following verbs are associated with human **emotions** and cognitive **feelings**
- In the **intransitive** form, they are used in the genitive case

Transitive	Intransitive (Genitive)	Meaning	Verb
	زما تبه شوه	to get a fever	تبه کېدل
	ستا يخ کيږي	to feel cold	يخ کېدل
	سارهٔ مي کيږي	to feel cold	سارهٔ کېدل
	دَ هغهٔ گرمي وَ شوه	to feel hot	گرمي کېدل
	تاودهٔ يې کيږي	to feel an urge	تاودهٔ کېدل
	خوا مي کيږي	to wish	خوا کېدل
	زړه دي کيږي	to wish	زړهٔ کېدل
موږ هوا وَکوله	زموږ هوا کيږي	to wish	هوا کېدل
تاسي هَوَس وَ کؤ	هَوَس مو کيږي	to wish	هَوَس کېدل
زه هغه ښه اېسم	ښه مي اېسي	to like	ښهٔ اېسېدل
زه هغهٔ بد اېسم	زما بد اېسي	to dislike	بد اېسېدل
هغوي راخُخه کوي	دَ هغوی کرکه راخُخه کيږي	to hate	کرکه کېدل
هغهٔ نفرت راخُخه کوي	نفرت يې راخُخه کيږي	to hate	نفرت کېدل
هغه ډار نه کوي	ډار يې نه کيږي	to scare from	ډار کېدل
هغهٔ وېره نهٔ کوي	وېره يې نهٔ کيږي	to fear	وېره کېدل
زه لمر خوښوم	زما لمر خوښيږي	to like	خوښېدل
زه په تا بد نهٔ لوروم	زما په تا بد نهٔ لوريږي	to wish	لورېدل
زه په تا بد نهٔ پهرزو کوم	په تا مي بد نهٔ پهرزو کيږي	to wish	پهرزو کېدل
ته ولې رخه کوې؟	ستا ولې رخه کيږي؟	to feel jelousy	رخه کېدل
ته ولې سيالي کوې؟	ستا ولې سيالي کيږي؟	to feel jelousy	سيالي کېدل
زه کور يادوم	کور مي ياديږي	to miss	يادېدل
زه هغه نه په زړه کوم	زما نه په زړه کيږي	to remember	په زړه کېدل
زه انگرېزي زده کوم	زما انگرېزي زده کيږي	to learn	زده کېدل
تا لوست هېر کؤ	ستا لوست هېر شؤ	to forget	هېرېدل

Adjectives

- In Pashto, adjectives are generally put before nouns
- They follow the same rules of gender, number and case as nouns
- They are divided into **four** main groups on the basis of their ending sounds: 1) consonants, 2) diphthongs, 3) ablaut, 4) vowels.
- It is convenient to first identify the ending sounds of Masculine and then change them into Feminine

For gender and plurality of adjectives, see the following tables (a) and (b):

(a) Formation of Feminine from Masculine

Examples		Masculine Endings changing into Feminine	Masculine Endings	No
Feminine	**Masculine**			
سپینه ښځه	سپین سړی	Masculine adjectives ending in **consonants** form their feminine by adding /ه/	Consonant	1
نـری ښځه	نـری سړی	**(i)** If the stress occurs on the letter immediately before /ی/, it is replaced by Feminine diphthong /ۍ/	**Masculine diphthong** /ی/	2
ښکـلې ښځه	ښکـلی سړی	**(ii)** If the stress does not occurs on the letter immediately before /ی/, it is replaced by **Feminine vowel** /ې/		
پنبتنه ښځه	پنبتـون سړی	In Masculine adjectives the *ablaut*, /و/ is dropped and the vowel of /ه/ is added	**Ablaut**	3
نیژدې ښځه	نیژدې سړی	- Adjectives ending in **vowels** /ه،/ /و،/ /ي/ and /ا/ are the same for Masculine and Feminine both	**Vowels**	4
نامتو ښځه	نامتو سړی			
واوه ښځه	واوه سړی			
اشنا ښځه	اشنا سړی	- the change of /ي/ into /ۍ/ is optional		
بازاريۍ ښځه	بازاري سړی			

(b) Formation of Plural adjectives from Singular

Feminine Plural	Feminine Singular	Masculine Plural	Masculine Singular	Alteration in ending sounds	No
سپينې ښځې	سپينه ښځه	سپين سړي	سپين سړی	*Masculine*: No alteration *Feminine*: /ه/, is replaced by /ي/	1
نـــرې ښځې ښکلي ښځې	نــرۍ ښځه ښکلي ښځه	نـرۍ سړي ښکلي سړي	نـرۍ سړی ښکلی سړی	*(a) Masculine*: /ی/ is replaced by /ي/ *Feminine*: No alteration in /ۍ/ *(b) Masculine*: /ی/ replaced by /ي/ *Feminine*: No alteration in /ۍ/	2
پښتنې ښځې	پښتنه ښځه	پښتانۀ سړي	پښتون سړی	*Masculine*: /و/ is replaced by /ا/ and vowel /ۀ/ is added *Feminine*: /و/ is dropped, and /ه/ to make a singular which is replaced by /ي/ in plural	3
واده ښځې اشنا ښځې نيژدي ښځې نامتو ښځې بازاري ښځې	واده ښځه اشنا ښځه نيژدي ښځه نامتو ښځه بازاري ښځه	واده سړي اشنا سړي نيژدي سړي نامتو سړي بازاري سړي	واده سړی اشنا سړی نيژدي سړی نامتو سړی بازاري سړی	*Masculine*: No alteration *Feminine*: No alteration	4

Exercises

(1) (<u>Adjectives ending in *consonants*</u>)

a) <u>**Masculine:**</u> same in singular and plural both

b) <u>**Feminine:**</u> to singulars a /ه/, while to plurals a /ي/ is added

Meaning	MS	MP	FS	FP
White	سپین	سپین	سپینه	سپینې
ready	تیار	تیار	تیاره	تیارې
Narrow	تنگ	تنگ	تنگه	تنگې
Tousled	جر	جر	جره	جرې
Whole	ټول	ټول	ټوله	ټولې
difficult	سخت	سخت	سخته	سختې
wide	پراخ	پراخ	پراخه	پراخې
Scattered	تیت	تیت	تیته	تیتې
black	تور	تور	توره	تورې
big	لوی	لوی	لویه	لویې
seated	ناست	ناست	ناسته	ناستې
Obliged	مجبور	مجبور	مجبوره	مجبورې
Known	مالوم	مالوم	مالومه	مالومې
Healthy	روغ	روغ	روغه	روغې
good	ښه	ښه	ښه	ښې
Bad	بد	بد	بده	بدې
Expensive	گران	گران	گرانه	گرانې
cheap	ارزان	ارزان	ارزانه	ارزانې
skinny	ډنگر	ډنگر	ډنگره	ډنگرې
tall	جگ	جگ	جگه	جگې
Short	لنډ	لنډ	لنډه	لنډې
wide	پراخ	پراخ	پراخه	پراخې
light	سپک	سپک	سپکه	سپکې
wise	پوه	پوه	پوهه	پوهې
Weak	سست	سست	سسته	سستې
Good	ښه	ښه	ښه	ښې
ugly	بدرنگ	بدرنگ	بدرنگه	بدرنگې

(2) (Adjectives *ending in diphthong* /ی/)

    i.   *Where stress happens* **immediately** *before* /ی/

        a) **Masculine**: the /ی/ in singular changes into the /ي/ in plurals

        b) **Feminine**: in both singulars and plurals it changes into /ۍ/

Meaning	MS	MP	FS	FP
Thin	نری	نري	نرۍ	نرۍ
round	گردی	گردي	گردۍ	گردۍ
Primary	لومړنی	لومړني	لومړنۍ	لومړنۍ
last	وروستی	وروستي	وروستۍ	وروستۍ
Mountainous	غرنی	غرني	غرنۍ	غرنۍ
Former	پخوانی	پخواني	پخوانۍ	پخوانۍ
Alive	ژوندی	ژوندي	ژوندۍ	ژوندۍ
small	کوچنی	کوچني	کوچنۍ	کوچنۍ

    ii.   *Where stress happens either in the* **beginning** *or in the* **middle** *of adjective but not immediately before* /ی/

        a) **Masculine**: the /ی/ in singulars changes into /ي/ in plurals

        b) **Feminine**: in both singulars and plurals it changes into /ې/

Meaning	MS	MP	FS	FP
New	نوی	نوي	نوې	نوې
beautiful	ښکلی	ښکلي	ښکلې	ښکلې
Hungry	وږی	وږي	وږې	وږې
Flaming	سوی	سوي	سوې	سوې
quiet	غلی	غلي	غلې	غلې
Thirsty	تږی	تږي	تږې	تږې
complex	پیچلی	پیچلي	پیچلې	پیچلې

(3) (<u>Adjectives having a</u> /و/ in the *middle*)

    a) <u>Masculine</u>: The /و/ in singulars changes into /ا/ in plurals and also a /ه/ is added at the end

    b) <u>Feminine</u>: In singulars /و/ is dropped altogether, however, a /ه/ is added at the end, while in plurals it is replaced by /ي/

Meaning	MS	MP	FS	FP
Lying	پروت	پراته	پرته	پرتي
ripe, mature	پوخ	پاخه	پخه	پخي
Soft	پوست	پاسته	پسته	پستي
hot	تود	تاوده	توده	تودي
spread	خپور	خپاره	خپره	خپري
sweat	خوړ	خواړه	خوړه	خوړي
Heavy	دروند	درانده/درانه	درنده/درنه	درندي/درني
Blind	روند	رانده	رنده	رندي
Old	زوړ	زاړه	زړه	زړي
mounted	سپور	سپاره	سپره	سپري
returnee	ستون	ستانه	ستنه	ستني
Cold	سوړ	ساړه	سړه	سړي
Uneven	کوږ	کاږه	کږه	کږي
deaf	کون	کانه	کنه	کني
wet	لوند	لانده	لنده	لندي
full (food)	موړ	ماړه	مړه	مړي
Small	ووړ	واړه	وړه	وړي
	وریت	ورتۀ	ورته	ورتي
	تریخ	ترخۀ	ترخه	ترخي
	تریو	تروۀ	تروه	تروي
	شین	شنۀ	شنه	شني
	سور	سرۀ	سره	سري

(4) (The _Unchangeable_ Adjectives) /و، ي، ا، ةَ/

Adjectives ending in the above sounds are unchangeable.

Meaning	MS	MP	FS	FP
famous	نامتو	نامتو	نامتو	نامتو
Near	نږدې	نږدې	نږدې	نږدې
Sure	ډاډه	ډاډه	ډاډه	ډاډه
familiar	اشنا	اشنا	اشنا	اشنا
upset	خپه	خپه	خپه	خپه
strong	تکړه	تکړه	تکړه	تکړه
Beautiful	ښايسته	ښايسته	ښايسته	ښايسته
simple	ساده	ساده	ساده	ساده
	سخي	سخي	سخي/سخی	سخي/سخی
	بازاري	بازاري	بازاري/بازاری	بازاري/بازاری

Adjective Exercises

Meaning	MS	MP	FS	FP
White	سپين			
ready	تيار			
Narrow	تنگ			
Tousled	جر			
Whole	ټول			
difficult	سخت			
wide	پراخ			
Scattered	تيت			
black	تور			
big	لوی			

59

seated	ناست			
Obliged	مجبور			
Known	مالوم			
Healthy	روغ			
good	ښه			
Bad	بد			
expensive	گران			
cheap	ارزان			
skinny	ډنگر			
tall	جگ			
Short	لنډ			
wide	پراخ			
light	سپک			
wise	پوه			
weak	سست			
good	ښه			
ugly	بدرنگ			

Meaning	MS	MP	FS	FP
Thin	نری			
round	گردی			
Primary	لومړنی			
last	وروستی			

Meaning		MP	FS	FP
mountainous	غرنی			
Former	پخوانی			
Alive	ژوندی			
small	کوچنی			

Meaning	MS	MP	FS	FP
New	نوی			
beautiful	ښکلی			
Hungry	وږی			
Flaming	سوی			
quiet	غلی			
Thirsty	تږی			
complex	پیچلی			

Meaning	MS	MP	FS	FP
Lying	پروت			
Ripe, mature	پوخ			
Soft	پوست			
hot	تود			
spread	خپور			
sweat	خوړ			
Heavy	دروند			
Blind	روند			
Old	زوړ			
mounted	سپور			
returnee	ستون			
Cold	سوړ			
Uneven	کوږ			
deaf	کوڼ			
wet	لوند			
full (food)	موړ			
Small	ووړ			
	وریت			
	تریخ			
	تریو			

Cases

Cases and Pre/Postpositions

- There are <u>ten</u> cases in Pashto
- All cases are formed by the use of pre-postpositions except **Nominative**, **Agentive** and **Accusative** cases

1.	Nominative	
2	Agentive	(as Subject always in the past tenses of transitive verbs)
3	Accusative	تا ، ما (as direct object only in present/ future tenses)
4	Vocative	to address others. يا ، يه، اى، وَ، is prefixed to nouns
5	Dative	ته = (to), لپاره (for)
6	Genitive	د , = (of and 's)
7	Ablative	له - څخه = from
8	Locative	له سره،په پسې،په په کښې ، په/پر باندې ، تر لاندې، پر سببره، تر پورې پورې،
9	Instrumental	په = by means of (an instrument)
10	Oblique plurals	وُ (is added to all plural nouns with transitive verbs)

Changeable Nouns

1. All the *masculine* nouns ending in the letter of /ى/ are changeable; and this letter changes into /ي/:

Examples: سړى= سړي، دوبى=دوبي، زلمى=زلمي

2. All the *feminine* nouns ending in the letter /ه/ are changeable; and is replaced by /ې/:

Examples: تخته=تختې، ونه=ونې، نسخه=نسخې

3. Generally the *monosyllabic* nouns are changeable and a /ه/ is added to them:

Examples: غل=غلهٔ، خر= خرهٔ، مړ=مړهٔ

4. Nouns having a /و/ in the middle are changeable; it is replaced by /l/ while a /ه/ is added at the end of the nouns:

Examples: پښتون=پښتانهٔ، پوخ=پاخهٔ، تود= تاودهٔ

62

5   Abstract feminine nouns ending in /ي/ change into /ی/

Examples: پاکي: پاکی، دوستي: دوستی.

6.   The following singular personal *pronouns* are changeable:

Examples:

Oblique	Direct
ما	زه
تا	ته
دۀ	دی
دي/ هغې/دغې	دا/هغه/دغه
چا	څوک
کومې	کوم

7.   Consonants and Diphthongs in Vocative, Locative and Ablative Cases

Masculine nouns ending in consonants and diphthongs generally accept /ـه/ in vocative and in **only** prepositional (locative & ablative) cases (تر) and (له). However, if **both** *pre* and *post* positions (تر -- پوري) and /له ---څخه/ are used then the change is not preferred. In changeable form a /ه/ is added to these nouns.

Examples: پلار: وَپلاره، له پلاره، تر پلاره

2. Unchangeable Nouns

Nouns ending in /ا/، /و/، /ی/and some adjectives ending in /ه/ are unchangeable in cases. *Examples*: داوه، نجلی، پښتو، نخا

Common inflected Nouns

| Plural | | Singular | | | | | | | | | | |
Oblique & Pre/Post positional ـــو	Direct (Nominative)	Instumentativ په	Ablative له خخه / له ـ ي	Locative په-کي پر-باندي تر-لاندي تر-پوري له-سره په-پسي	Possessive د	Dative ته	Accusative (1rst & 2nd persons as object in present and future)	Vocative و/ای په ا/	Agentive (as subject with a transitive verb in past tense)	Direct (Nominative) Case	Endings	NO
سرو	سري	په سري	له سري څخه	سري	د سري	سري ته		و سريه !	سري کار وکؤ	سری	ی	1
ښنځو	ښنځي	په ښنځي	له ښنځي څخه	ښنځي	د ښنځي	ښنځي ته		اي ښنځي !	ښنځي کار وکؤ	ښنځه	ه	2
غلو	غله	په غله	له غله څخه	غله	د غله	غله ته	يه غله !	غله	غله کار وکؤ	غل	Mono syllable	3
پښتنو	پښتانه	په پښتانه	له پښتانه څخه	پښتانه	د پښتانه	پښتانه ته	و پښتونه ! اي کونه!	پښتانه	پښتانه کار وکؤ	پښتون	ablaut و	4
										دوستي	ي	5
		په ما، تا، ده، دي، چا	له ما، تا، ده، دي، چا	ما، تا، ده، دي، چا	د ما، تا، ده، دي، چا	ما، تا، ده، دي، چا ته	زه ما وهم ته ما وهي		ما، تا، ده، دي چا کار وکؤ	زه، ته دی، دا څوک	Pronouns Singular	6

64

Inflection of Nouns ending in consonants

Plural		Singular										N O
		Pre/postpositional Cases					Oblique Cases			Direct		
Obliq ue & Pre/Po st positio nal ـــو	Direct (Nominative)	Instumen tativ په	Ablati ve له ـ څخه له ـ راهيسي Optio nal but preferr ed	Locat ive په ـ کي پر ـ باندي تر ـ لاندي تر ـ پوري له ـ سره په ـ پسي Only optio nal له ـ سره تر ـ پوري	Posses sive د	Dati ve ته	Accusa tive (1rst & 2nd persons as object in present and future)	Vocat ive و/ ای یه /ا	Agent ive (as subjec t with a transit ive verb in past tense)	Direct (Nomina tive) Case	Endings	N O
	Direct (Nominative)		له ـ تر پلاره دوښمنه توپکه اسه هلکه مچه ماره چونگا ښه کبه له ـ پو دي	لهﺎتر پلاره دوښمنه توپکه اسه هلکه مچه ماره چونگا ښه کبه سره/ يو دي				پلاره! دوښمنه ! توپکه! اسه! هلکه! مچه! ماره! چونگا ښه! کبه!		پلار دوښمن توپک اس هلک مچ مار چونگابښ کب	Consonants	7

65

Inflection of Nouns ending in diphthongs

Plural		Singular										
Obliq ue & Pre/Po st positio nal و---	Direct (Nominative)	Pre/postpositional Cases					Oblique Cases			Direct (Nomina tive) Case	Endings (Diphthongs)	N O
		Instumen tativ په	Ablati ve له--- څخه له--- راهيسي Optio nal but prefer red	Locativ e په-کي پر- باندي تر- لاندي په - پسي تر- پوري له - سره Only option al the followi ng: تر- پوري له - سره	Posses sive د	Dati ve ته	Accusa tive (1rst & 2nd persons as object in present and future)	Vocat ive و/اي يه ا/	Agent ive (as subjec t with a transit ive verb in past tense)			
			لويه	لويه				لويه!		لوى	(وى)	
			خدايه	خدايه				خدايه!		خداى	(اى)	8
			پاياوه	پاياوه				پاياوه!		پاياو	(او)	
			پلوه	پلوه				پلوه!		پلو	(...َ و)	

66

Future Tense

Future Perfective (Simple) Tense:

- In Pashto both present and future tenses are identical to each other, and have almost the same rules,
- The only difference is the addition of the modal/future marker / به/ which means will/shall
- For all 3rd persons irrespective of their number and gender only *to be* of /وي/ is used.

Pronouns and *to be* in Future and Present Tense:

To be Future Tense		To be Present Tense	Pronoun
يم	به	يم	زه
يو	به	يو	موږ
يې	به	يې	ته
يئ	به	يئ	تاسي
وي	به	وي(دی)	دی/هغه
وي	به	وي(ده)	دا/هغه
وي	به	وي(دي)	دوی/هغوی

Comparison of Future and Present tense:

Future		Present		Verb Category	No
Imperfective	Perfective	Imperfective	Perfective		
زه وهم	زه به و وهم	زه وهم	زه و وهم	Simple Verb وهل	1
زه به خالي کوم زه به خالي کېږم زه به جوړوم زه به جوړېږم	زه به خالي کـم زه به خالي شـم زه به جوړ کـم زه به جوړ شـم	زه خالي کوم زه خالي کېږم زه جوړوم زه جوړېږم	زه خالي کـم زه خالي شـم زه جوړ کـم زه جوړ شـم	Long Compound Verb خالي کول/جوړول خالي کېدل/جوړېدل	2
زه به وړوم زه به وړېږم	زه به و وړوم زه به و وړېږم	زه وړوم زه وړېږم	زه و وړوم زه و وړېږم	Short Compound Verbs وړول/وړېدل	3
زه به پوري وهم	زه به پوري وهم	زه پوري وهم	زه پوري وهم	Shifting Stress پوري وهل	4

Perfect Tense

For any perfect tense, the use of **past participle** it is necessary

Past Participle

Past participle is formed from infinitive after adding one of the following: /ی/، /ي/، /ي/

- ی is added for masculine **singular**
- ي id added for masculine **plural**
- ي is added for feminine **singular** and **feminine**

Note:

- Only in the long compound verbs the auxiliaries: کول/کېدل and کول/کول change into کړ and شَو, respectively
- The adjectival/nominal part is declined according to the number and gender of the **subject** and **object** in **intransitive** and **transitive** verbs respectively
- No changes occur in the verbs of other categories.

For details see the following table:

Feminine		Masculine		4 Verb Categories	
Plural ي	Singular ي	Plural ي	Singular ی		
تللي	تللې	تللي	تللی	تلل	1
جوړې کړې	جوړه کړې	جوړ کړي	جوړ کړی	جوړول	2
جوړې شوې	جوړه شوې	جوړ شوي	جوړ شوی	جوړېدل	
وهرولي	وهرولې	وهرولي	وهرولی	وهرول	3
وهربدلي	وهربدلې	وهربدلي	وهربدلی	وهربدل	
کنبېناستلي	کنبېناستلې	کنبېناستلي	کنبېناستلی	کنبېناستل	4

Ergative construction

- As in other past tenses, in perfect tenses **Intransitive** past participles and *to be* also always agree with the **subject**
- However, with **transitive** past participles the **ergative** construction is used; in which the past participle and *to be* both agree with the **object**, which is put in direct case while the **subject** is used in *oblique* case

For further details see the following:

1. **Intransitive verb:** *To be* (agrees with S) + Past Participle (agree with S) + Subject

2. **Transitive verb:** *To be* (agrees with O) + Past Participle (agree with O) + Object + Subject *(oblique)*

1. Intransitive verb /تلل/

To be (Agreeing with the Subject)		Past Participle (Agreeing with the Subject)		Subject
Past Tense	Present Tense	Feminineي	Masculineی/ي	
وم	یم	تللې	تللی	زه
وو	یو	تللې	تللي	موږ
وې	یې	تللې	تللی	ته
وئ	یئ	تللې	تللي	تاسي
ؤ/وه	دی/ده	تللې	تللی	دی/دا
وې/ول	دي/دي	تللې	تللي	دوی

1. Transitive verb /وهل/

To be (Agreeing with the Object)		Past Participle (Agreeing with the Object)		Object	Subject (oblique)
Past Tense	Present Tense	Feminineي	Masculineی/ي		
وم	یم	وهلې	وهلی	زه	سري
وو	یو	وهلې	وهلي	موږ	سري
وې	یې	وهلې	وهلی	ته	سري
وئ	یئ	وهلې	وهلي	تاسي	سري
ؤ/وه	دی/ده	وهلې	وهلی	دی/دا	سري
وې/ول	دي/دي	وهلې	وهلي	دوی	سري

Future Perfect Tense

The rules of Present perfect tense and Future perfect tense are the same, apart from the following two features of the Future perfect tense:

(a) After the subject (the model) /به/ is added

(b) The *to be* /وي/ is used for all third persons irrespective of their gender and number

Passive Voice

- In the passive voice, the main verb is added by the verb /کېدل/ which is conjugated according to the tense and aspect
- The main verb is generally used in the *uninflected* **infinitive** (*plural masculine*) form: e.g. وهل کېدل: (to be beaten)
- After the subject (the actual acting person) the descriptive phrase: /لخوا/ is used
- Predicate inflects only the gender and number of the **object** in all tenses
- Object happens in the beginning of the sentence

Passive Voice Structure:

to be + کېدل + Verb + لخوا+ دَ +Subject+ دَ + Object

For the conjugation of the auxiliary /کېدل/ to the four categories of verb, see the following tables:

(1) Four categories of the main verbs used in active and passive forms:

Passive	Active
وهل كېدل	وهل
جوړول كېدل	جوړول
وېرول كېدل	وېرول
پوري وهل كېدل	پوري وهل

(2) The auxiliary verb /كېدل/

Past		Present		Verb
Imperfective	Perfective	Imperfective	Perfective (*Aorist*)	---------- + كېدل
---------- + كېدل	---------- + شوَ	---------- + كېږ	---------- + ش	

(3) The auxiliary verb /كېدل/ combined with the four categories of the main verbs:

Past		Present		Verb
Imperfective	Perfective	Imperfective	Perfective (*Aorist*)	
زه وهل كېدلم	زه وَوهل شوَم I was pushed	زه وهل كېږم I am being beaten	(كه) زه وَوهل شــم (*should*) I be beaten	وهل
زه جوړول كېدلم (زه جوړېدلم*) I was being made	زه جوړ كړل/كړ شوَم (زه جوړ شوم*) I was made	زه جوړول كېږم (زه جوړېږم*) I am being made	زه جوړ كړل/كړ شــم (زه جوړ شم*) (*should*) I be made	جوړول
زه وېرول كېدلم I was being frightened	زه وَ وېرول شوَم	زه وېرول كېږم I am being frightened	زه وَ وېرول شــم (*should*) I be frightened	وېرول
زه پوري وهل كېدلم I was being pushed	زه پوري وهل شوَم	زه پوري وهل كېږم I am being pushed	زه پوري وهل شــم (*should*) I be pushed	پوري وهل

* Colloquially, the long compound verbs are used in passive voice same as intransitive verbs in active voice

Moods

Potential Tenses

a. (Active Voice)

- The potential form is constructed by adding only /ای/ to the infinitive of a conjugating verb for all persons, irrespective of their number and gender
- It is followed by the auxiliary verb /شول/ which is inflected for person, number and gender
- In **present** tense, the auxiliary very /شول/ is used simply as /ـش/ while in the **past** tense it is can be used as /شوَ/
- In sentences with transitive verbs, the ergative construction is used
- Like other moods of Pashto language, the potential mood also has perfective and imperfective aspects
- In the transitive long compound verb the auxiliary /کول/changes into /کړلای/ or /کړای/when used in perfective aspect

_to be_ + /شوَ / ـش_   +   Verb+ /ای/   +   (_object_)   + Subject

See the verb /چیښل/ to drink in the following table:

Past		Present		Pronoun
Imperfective	**Perfective**	**Imperfective**	**Perfective**	
ما اوبه چیښلای شوَي	ما اوبه وَ چیښلای شوَي	زه اوبه چیښلای شم	(که) زه اوبه وَ چیښلای شم	1st S
I could drink water	I could drink water	I can drink water	(_should_) I can drink water	
موږ اوبه چیښلای شوَي	موږ اوبه وَ چیښلای شوَي	موږ اوبه چیښلای شو	(که) موږ اوبه وَ چیښلای شو	1st P
.we could drink water	We could drink water	we can drink water	(_should_) we can drink water	
تا اوبه چیښلای شوَي	تا اوبه وَ چیښلای شوَي	ته اوبه چیښلای شي	(که) ته اوبه وَ چیښلای شي	2nd S
you could drink water	you could drink water	you can drink water	(_should_) you can drink water	
تاسي اوبه چیښلای شوَي	تاسي اوبه وَ چیښلای شوَي	تاسي اوبه چیښلای شئ	(که) تاسي اوبه وَ چیښلای شئ	2nd P
.you could drink water	you could drink water	you can drink water	(_should_) you can drink water	
دۀ/دي/دوی اوبه چیښلای شوَي	دۀ/دي/دوی اوبه وَ چیښلای شوَي	دی/دا/دوی اوبه چیښلای شي	(که) دی/دا/دوی اوبه وَ چیښلای شي	3rd S/P
He/she/they could drink water	He/she/they could drink water	he/she/they can drink water	(_should_) he/she/they/ can drink water	

b. (Passive Voice)

- In both Present and Past **imperfective** tense to the infinitive of a conjugating verb /کیدلای/ is added for all persons, irrespective of their number and gender
- The Present passive perfective is the same as the Present active, the only difference is in the passive it the object which conjugates unlike in the active voice in which subject conjugates

_to be_ + /شوَ / ـش_   +   Verb+ /ای، کیدلای/   +   (لخوا+ _Subject_+دَ)   + Object

71

Past		Present		Pronoun
Imperfective	Perfective	Imperfective	Perfective (*Aorist*)	
زه دَ هغهٔ لخوا وهل کېدلای شوَم	زه دَ هغهٔ لخوا وَ وهلای شوَم	زه دَ هغهٔ لخوا وهل کېدلای شم	(کهٔ) زه دَ هغهٔ لخوا وَ وهلای شم	1st S
I could be beaten by him	I could be beaten by him	I can be beaten by him	(*should*) I can be beaten by him	
موږ دَ هغهٔ لخوا وهل کېدلای شوو	موږ دَ هغهٔ لخوا وَ وهلای شوو	موږ دَ هغهٔ لخوا وهل کېدلای شو	(کهٔ) موږ دَ هغهٔ لخوا وَ وهلای شو	1st P
we could be beaten by him	We could be beaten by him	we can be beaten by him	(*should*) we can be beaten by him	
ته دَ هغهٔ لخوا وهل کېدلای شوَې	ته دَ هغهٔ لخوا وَ وهلای شوَې	ته دَ هغهٔ لخوا وهل کېدلای شې	(کهٔ) ته دَ هغهٔ لخوا وَ وهلای شې	2nd S
you could be beaten by him	you could be beaten by him	you can be beaten by him	(*should*) you can be beaten by him	
تاسې دَ هغهٔ لخوا وهل کېدلای شوَئ	تاسې دَ هغهٔ لخوا وَ وهلای شوَئ	تاسې دَ هغهٔ لخوا وهل کېدلای شئ	(کهٔ) تاسې دَ هغهٔ لخوا وَ وهلای شئ	2nd P
you could be beaten by him	you could be beaten by him	you can be beaten by him	(*should*) you can be beaten by him	
دی دَ هغهٔ لخوا وهل کېدلای شؤ	دی دَ هغهٔ لخوا وَ وهلای شؤ	دی/دا/دوی دَ هغهٔ لخوا وهل کېدلای شي	(کهٔ) دی/دا/دوی دَ هغهٔ لخوا وَ وهلای شي	3rd S/P
دا دَ هغهٔ لخوا وهل کېدلای شوَه	دا دَ هغهٔ لخوا وَ وهلای شوَه		(*should*) he/she/they/ can be beaten by him	
دوی دَ هغهٔ لخوا وهل کېدلای شوَی	دوی دَ هغوی لخوا وَ وهلای شول			
دوی دَ هغهٔ لخوا وهل کېدلای شوي	دوی دَ هغهٔ لخوا وَ وهلای شوي	he/she/they can be beaten by him		
he/she/they could be beaten by him	He/she/they could be beaten by him			

Optative Mood

(a) Active Voice:

- By using /کهٔ/، /کاشکي/، /پکار ده/ at the beginning of the Present **Indicative** mood it changes into the *subjunctive*, *Optative* and *conditional* moods
- In the Past tense /ای/ is added to the main verb and used impersonally. (*Though it has the structure of Past tense, it is also used for Present tense*)

Present tense

to be +Verb   +   (*Obj*)   +   Sub+ کاشکي

Past/Present tense

/ای/ +Verb   +   (*Obj*)   +   Sub+ کاشکي

72

	Past/Present		Present		Verb
Imperfective	**Perfective**	**Imperfective**	**Perfective (Aorist)**		
/اکه/، /کاشکي/، /پکار ده/ما کار کولای	/اکه/، /کاشکي/، /پکار ده/ما کار	/اکه/، /کاشکي/، /پکار ده/زه کار	/اکه/، /کاشکي/، /پکار ده/ زه کار		۱ کول
/اکه/، /کاشکي/، /پکار ده/کار کبدلای	وَ کولای	کوم	کارو کوم		کېدل
	/اکه/، /کاشکي/، /پکار ده/کار وَ	/اکه/، /کاشکي/، /پکار ده/کار	/اکه/، /کاشکي/، /پکار ده/ کار وَ		
	شوای	کیږي	شي		
/اکه/، /کاشکي/، /پکار ده/ما کار جوړولای	/اکه/، /کاشکي/، /پکار ده/ما کار	/اکه/، /کاشکي/، /پکار ده/زه کار	/اکه/، /کاشکي/، /پکار ده/زه کار		۲ جوړول
/اکه/، /کاشکي/، /پکار ده/کار جوړېدلای	جوړ کړای	جوړوم	جوړ کم		جوړېدل
	/اکه/، /کاشکي/، /پکار ده/کار	/اکه/، /کاشکي/، /پکار ده/ کار	/اکه/، /کاشکي/، /پکار ده/ کار		
	جوړ شوای	جوړېږي	جوړ شي		
/اکه/، /کاشکي/، /پکار ده/ زه کښېناستلای	/اکه/، /کاشکي/، /پکار ده/زه	/اکه/، /کاشکي/، /پکار ده/زه	/اکه/، /کاشکي/، /پکار ده/زه		۳
/اکه/، /کاشکي/، /پکار ده/ما ته کښېنولای	کښېناستلای	کښېنم	کښېنم		کښېناستل
	/اکه/، /کاشکي/، /پکار ده/ما ته	/اکه/، /کاشکي/، /پکار ده/زه تا	/اکه/، /کاشکي/، /پکار ده/زه تا		کښېنول
	کښېنولای	کښېنوم	کښېنوم		
/اکه/، /کاشکي/، /پکار ده/ما رباب شرنګولای	/اکه/، /کاشکي/، /پکار ده/ما	/اکه/، /کاشکي/، /پکار ده/زه	/اکه/، /کاشکي/، /پکار ده/زه		۴ شرنګول
/اکه/، /کاشکي/، /پکار ده/رباب شرنګېدلای	رباب وَشرنګولای	رباب شرنګوم	رباب وَشرنګوم		شرنګېدل
	/اکه/، /کاشکي/، /پکار ده/ رباب	/اکه/، /کاشکي/، /پکار ده/رباب	/اکه/، /کاشکي/، /پکار ده/ رباب		
	وَشرنګېدلای	شرنګېږي	وَشرنګېږي		

(b)   *Passive Voice:*

- At the begging of the tense /اکه/، /کاشکي/، /پکار ده/ is used
- In the Present tense /ای/ is added to the main verb; and in the end /ـش/ is conjugated
  in the Perfective while /کیږ/ in the Imperfective aspect
- In Past tense /شوای/ is used in the Perfective while /کبدلای/ in the Imperfective aspect

	Past/Present		Present		Verb
Imperfective	**Perfective**	**Imperfective**	**Perfective (Aorist)**		
/اکه/، /کاشکي/، /پکار ده/کار دَ هغه لخوا	/اکه/، /کاشکي/، /پکار ده/کار دَ هغه	/اکه/، /کاشکي/، /پکار ده/کار دَ هغه لخوا	/اکه/، /کاشکي/، /پکار ده/کار دَ هغه		۱ کول
کول کبدلای	لخوا وَ کول شوای	کولای کیږي	لخوا وَ کولای شي		
(کار دَ هغه لخوا کبدلای)		(کار دَ هغه لخوا کیږي)			
/اکه/، /کاشکي/، /پکار ده/کار دَ هغه لخوا	/اکه/، /کاشکي/، /پکار ده/ کار دَ هغه	/اکه/، /کاشکي/، /پکار ده/کار دَ هغه لخوا	/اکه/، /کاشکي/، /پکار ده/کار دَ هغه		۲ جوړول
جوړول کبدلای	لخوا جوړ کړای شوای	جوړولای کیږي	لخوا جوړ کړای شي		
(کار دَ هغه لخوا جوړېدلای)		(کار دَ هغه لخوا جوړېږي)			
/اکه/، /کاشکي/، /پکار ده/زه دَ هغه لخوا	/اکه/، /کاشکي/، /پکار ده/زه دَ هغه	/اکه/، /کاشکي/، /پکار ده/زه دَ هغه	/اکه/، /کاشکي/، /پکار ده/زه دَ هغه		۳
کښېنول کبدلای	لخوا کښېنول شوای	لخوا کښېنولای کیږم	لخوا کښېنولای شم		کښېنول
/اکه/، /کاشکي/، /پکار ده/رباب شرنګول	/اکه/، /کاشکي/، /پکار ده/رباب دَ	/اکه/، /کاشکي/، /پکار ده/رباب دَ هغه	/اکه/، /کاشکي/، /پکار ده/رباب دَ		۴
کبدلای	هغه لخوا وَشرنګول شوای	لخوا شرنګولای کیږي	هغه لخوا وَشرنګولای شي		شرنګول
(رباب شرنګبدلای)		/اکه/، /کاشکي/، /پکار ده/رباب دَ هغه			
		لخوا شرنګېږي			

73

The Potential-Optative Mood

- The Present Potential-Optative tense is same as the present potential tense except in the former a sentence begins with كاش، كاشكي، كاشكي چي، ارمان
- The Past potential-optative tense is also the same as potential tense except the use of ارمان چي، كاشكي، كاش/كه in the beginning of the sentence and the auxiliary شوای/ at the end of the sentence for **all pronouns**. *(Though it has the structure of Past tense, it is also used for the Present tense)*

Present tense

to be+ شـ   +   ای/ای+Verb   +   (Obj)   +   Sub+كاشكي

Past/Present tense

شوای   +   ای/ای+Verb   +   (Obj)   +   Sub+كاشكي

(a) Active Voice:

Past/Present		Present		Verb
Imperfective	Perfective	Imperfective	Perfective	
كاشكي ما كار كولای شوای / كاشكي كار كپدل شوای	كاشكي ما كار وَ كولای شوای / كاشكي كار وَكپدل شوای	كاشكي زه كار كولای شم / كاشكي كار كپدلای شي	كاشكي زه كار وَكولای شم / كاشكي كار وَكپدلای شي	1كول كپدل
كاشكي ما كار جوړولای شوای / كاشكي كار جوړېدلای شوای	كاشكي ما كار جوړ كړای شوای / كاشكي كار جوړ شوای	كاشكي زه كار جوړ ولای شم / كار كار جوړ ېدلای شي	كاشكي زه كار جوړ كړای شم / كاشكي كار جوړ شي	2جوړول جوړېدل
كاشكي زه كښېناستلای شوای / كاشكي ما ته كښېنولای شوای	كاشكي زه كښېناستلای شوای / كاشكي ما ته كښېنولای شوای	كاشكي زه كښېناستلای شم / كاشكي زه تا كښېنولای شم	كاشكي زه كښېناستلای شم / كاشكي زه تا كښېنولای شم	3كښېناستل كښېنول
كاشكي ما رباب شرنگولای شوای / كاشكي رباب شرنگېدلای شوای	كاشكي ما رباب وَشرنگولای شوای / كاشكي رباب وَشرنگېدلای شوای	كاشكي زه رباب شرنگولای شم / كاشكي رباب شرنگېدلای شي	كاشكي زه رباب وَشرنگولای شم / كاشكي رباب وَشرنگېدلای شي	4شرنگول شرنگېدل

(b) Passive Voice:

Past/Present		Present		Verb
Imperfective	Perfective	Imperfective	Perfective	
كاشكي كار دَ هغه لخوا كول كپدلای شوای (كاشكي كار دَ هغه لخوا كپدلای شوای)	كاشكي كار دَ هغه لخوا وَ كولی شوای	كاشكي كار دَ هغه لخوا كول كپدلای شي (كاشكي كار دَ هغه لخوا كپدلای شي)	كاشكي كار دَ هغه لخوا وَ كولای شي	1كول
كاشكي كار دَ هغه لخوا جوړول كپدلای شوای (كاشكي كار دَ هغه لخوا جوړ پدلای شوای)	كاشكي كار دَ هغه لخوا جوړ كړای شوای	كاشكي كار دَ هغه لخوا جوړول كپدلای شي (كاشكي كار دَ هغه لخوا جوړ پدلای شي)	كاشكي كار دَ هغه لخوا جوړ كړای شي	2جوړول
كاشكي زه دَ هغه لخوا كښېنول كپدلای شوای	كاشكي زه دَ هغه لخوا كښېنولای شوای	كاشكي زه دَ هغه لخوا كښېنول كپدلای شم	كاشكي زه دَ هغه لخوا كښېنولای شم	3كښېنول
كاشكي رباب شرنگول كپدلای شوای (كاشكي رباب شرنگېدلای شوای)	كاشكي رباب دَ هغه لخوا وَشرنگولای شوای	كاشكي رباب دَ هغه لخوا شرنگول كپدلای شي / كاشكي رباب دَ هغه لخوا شرنگېدلای شي	كاشكي رباب دَ هغه لخوا وَشرنگولای شي	4شرنگول

The Past Perfect tense and different moods

(a) Active Voice

By adding کاشکي/، /که/، پکارده/ at the beginning and //وای in the end of the Past perfect tense, it changes in to the *subjunctive*, *optative* and *conditional* moods, e.g.:

پکارده/کاشکي/که زه راغلی وای

پکارده/کاشکي/که ما ډوډی خوړلې وای

پکارده/کاشکي/که تاسي لوبه کړې وای

(b) Passive Voice

Add پکارده/، /کاشکي/، /که/ in the beginning, conjugate شول/ after the main verb and add وای/ at the end, e.g.:

پکارده/کاشکي/که زه راوستل شوی وای

پکارده/کاشکي/که ډوډی خوړل شوې وای

پکارده/کاشکي/که لوبه کول شوې وای (لوبه شوې وای)

The Use of *model* (بـــــــه) will/shall/ would/ may/might/ should:

Apart from future tense model (به) is used in various other contexts:

1. Habitual Present

ته کار راته کوه، زه به کیسې درته کوم

You carry on working, I am telling the stories.

2. Habitual/Perpetual Past

ما به پروسږ کال هره ورځ ښکار کولؤ

Last year, I used to/would hunt every day

3. Doubtful Past

In Pashto the Future Perfect is also used as doubtful past:

(کېدلای شي) لونګ بـــه زما رباب غلا کړی وي

It is possible that/perhaps *Lawung* has stolen my guitar

4. **Reprehensive Past**

It is used to express regret or reprimand about an action that did not take place, which should have been done. It is used in past **imperfective** and **pluperfect** tense. Some times for more emphasis particle /خو/ is also added

هغه زما مرسته و نه کوله، تا خو به کوله (تا خو به کړې وه)

He did not help me, you should have helped me.

5. **Conditional**

If you will be there, I will come	که ته هلته وې ، (نو) زه به هم درشم
If you are there, I will also come.	که ته هلته يې، (نو) زه به هم درشم
If you were there, I would (used) to come.	که به ته هلته وې، (نو) زه به هم درغلم
If you used to be there, I used to come	که به ته هلته وې (نو) زه به هم درتلم
Had you been there, I would have com	که ته هلته وای، (نو) زه به هم درغلی وم
If I were fine, I would have done it	که زه جوړ وای نو ما به دا کار کړی و.

The Imperative Mood *(2ⁿᵈ Person)*

- Generally the imperative mood is in the 2ⁿᵈ person singular and plural. In singular /ه/ while in plural /ئ/ is added after the verb.
- The **four** main categories of verb follow the rules of present tense in both perfective and imperfective aspects.
- In the perfective aspect, the nominal part of transitive verbs agrees with the direct object.
- With the negative – prohibitive particle /مه/ is added before verb, and it is always used only in **perfective** aspect.

Negative (Plural)	(Singular)	Positive (Singular) Imperfective (Final Stress)	Perfective (Initial Stress)	Positive (Plural) Imperfective (Final Stress)	Perfective (Initial Stress)	Verb Categories	No
تاسي باجه مه وهئ	ته باجه مه وه	تاسي باجه و وهئ	تاسي باجه وهئ	ته باجه وهه	ته باجه و وهه	**Simple** وهل	1
تاسي کوټه مه پاکوئ تاسي مه پاکېږئ تاسي کوټه مه جوړوئ تاسي مه جوړېږئ	ته کوټه مه پاکوه ته مه پاکېږه ته کوټه مه جوړوه ته مه جوړېږه	تاسي کوټه پاکوئ تاسي پاک شئ تاسي کوټه جوړوئ تاسي جوړ شئ	تاسي کوټه پاکه کئ تاسي پاک شئ تاسي کوټه جوړه کئ تاسي جوړ شئ	ته کوټه پاکوه ته پاکېږه ته کوټه جوړوه ته جوړېږه	ته کوټه پاکه که ته پاک شه ته کوټه جوړه که ته جوړ شه	**Long** Compound پاکول/جوړول پاکېدل/جوړېدل	2
تاسي پیشو مه وبروئ تاسي مه وبرېږئ	ته پیشو مه وبروه ته مه وبرېږه	تاسي پیشو و وبروئ تاسي و وبرېږئ	تاسي پیشو و بروئ تاسي و برېږئ	ته پیشو و بروه ته و برېږه	ته پیشو و بروه ته و برېږه	**Short** Compound وبرول/وبرېدل	3
تاسي دروازه مه پوري وهئ	ته دروازه مه پوري وهه	تاسي دروازه پوري وهئ	تاسي دروازه پوري وهئ	ته دروازه پوري وهه	ته دروازه پوري وهه	**Shifting Stress** پوري وهل	4

The Imperative mood and the use of /دي/: (*Let, Should*)

Apart from being a weak pronoun for the 2nd person, /دي/ is also used as a particle in imperative mood in the following contexts:

1   Order/ Suggestion

Let him come/ He should come	هغه دي راشي
Let you come/ You should come	ته دي راشې
Let me come/ I should come	زه دي راشم

2   Threat/emphasis/promise

(Should) you go I will see you	ته(خو)دي ورشې!، (زه به ورسره جوړ شم)
(First) you should go I will help you	دی (خو) دي ورشي/ورشې!، (نو زه به مرسته ورسره وکوم)

3   Speculative

I don't think I may (will) go there.	ګومان نه کوم چې زه دي ورشم
It is impossible that you have gone there	ناشونې ده، چې ته دي ورغلی يې

4   Comparison

Should I do this, then see the result.	زه دي دغه کار وکوم، نو بيا يې پايله وګوره.

5   Perhaps/possibly:

This year the Labour party will win?	سږکال به کارګر ګوند بريالی شي؟
Yes, perhaps/possibly	هو، وَ دي شي.

6   Blessing/Cursing

May God rain!	خدای دي باران وکوي!
May God kill him!	خدای دي هغه مړ کي،.
Down with	مړ دي وي،
Long live!	ژوندی دي وي، تل دي وي!

7   Weak Pronouns

In the sentences of blessing or cursing when weak pronouns are used as a direct object, the location of the particle /دي/varies from person to person; with 1st person, it is used **before** the weak pronoun, with 3rd person, **after** the weak pronoun, and with the 2nd person it is **not** used at all

May God help me!	خدای مي دي مرسته وَ کوي
May God help him/her/them!	خدای دي يې مرسته وَ کوي

8   However, without the particle /دي/ the ending /ي/ is replaced by /ه/:

May God help us!	خدای مو مرسته وَکوه
May God help him/her/them!	خدای یې مرسته وَکوه
May God help you!	خدای دي مرسته وَکوه
May God bring you (welcome)	خدا دي راوله
May God bring you (welcome)	خدای مو راوله

9   If in these sentences the verb is intransitive, the 2nd person singular ends in /ي/ and plural in /ئ/

	Plural	Singular
May you not be tired!	ستړی مه شئ	ستړی مه شې
May you come in peace!	پخیر راشئ	پخیر راشې
May you come any time!	هر کله راشئ	هر کله راشې
May you be prosperous!	اباد اوسئ	اباد اوسې
May you be healthy!	روغ اوسئ	روغ اوسې

79

References:

1. Zyar Majawir Ahmad, *Pashto Grammar*, Danish Publishing Association1384

2. Cox A. D. *Notes on Pashto Grammar,* Asian Educational Services New Dehli, Madras, 2001

3. Abid Khan Zain-ul-Abidin, *Every – Day Pushtu,* Asian Educational Services New Dehli, Madras, 2005

4. Khan Qazi Rhimullah, *Introduction to Pushtu*, Hippocrene Books, INC. 171 Madison Avenue New York, NY 10016

5. Shafeev D.A. *A Short Grammatical Outline of Pashto*, Indiana Univesity, Bloomington Mount & Co, The Hague, The Nehterlands 1964

6. Tegey, Habibullah; Robson, Barbera, *A Reference Grammar of Pashto*, Center for Applied Linguistics, Washington, D.C. 1996

7. Roberts Taylor, *Clitics and Agreement, Massachusetts Institute of Technology*, 2000

8. Rishtin Sidiqullah, *Pashto Grammar*, Pashto Tolana Kabul Afghanistan